Contents

Preface

The human brain is like a muscle, which needs to be exercised to stay in good condition. Not just any exercise either. Experts say the best mental exercise involves challenging the brain in new ways. In other words, while it's fine to reinforce and strengthen existing ways of thinking, it's even better to build new ones.

For a good, fresh, all-round mental workout — one you'll enjoy, too — it would be hard to do better than the puzzles in this book. All of them are from the World Puzzle Championship, an annual event, or are new puzzles (based on WPC types) created especially for this volume. You may be familiar with a few of the types already, such as Sudoku or Battleships (usually with a twist here). But most of the types will probably be new. Your brain is about to be stretched in ways you've never imagined!

Founded in 1992 in New York, the World Puzzle Championship is held in a different city and country every year. All the puzzles in the event are language- and culture-neutral, so that people from every part of the world can compete equally. For more information on the WPC, including how to try out for your national team that will compete at the event, see www.worldpuzzle.org.

Meanwhile, get a pencil, settle back in your favorite puzzle-solving chair ... and turn the page!

W m Shortz

Will Shortz

═══ How to Use This Book ═══

This book has 151 puzzles, divided into three sections by approximate difficulty: Training Puzzles (about half of the book), National Puzzles (about 25%), and World-Class Puzzles (the last 25%). Within each section there are 22 puzzle types, with similar puzzle types grouped together. (The detailed list of types can be found on page 2.)

If this is your first time solving puzzles like these, we recommend simply starting at the beginning and doing the puzzles in order; whenever a new puzzle type is introduced, instructions and a simple example are given with the first Training Puzzle. Of course, you are free to skip over any puzzles or puzzle types that you are not interested in.

A few puzzles refer to a Tutorial in the back of the book. If you are having trouble getting started on a puzzle, the Tutorial will give you some tips and techniques on getting started. Some puzzles may have a specific "sticking point" where it is difficult to make progress if you don't see a certain feature. Those puzzles will refer to a "hint available" in the back of the book.

At the bottom of each puzzle page is a note telling you which page to find the solution for that puzzle. The puzzle solutions are on the pages in an interweaving order, so when you look at a solution you are unlikely to accidentally see the answer to the previous or subsequent puzzle.

Finally, each puzzle has three target times next to it. The "Par" time is our best guess on how long an average solver will take to solve the puzzle; the "Expert" time is an estimate of how long an average participant at the WPC would take; and the "Record" time is the best time logged among all of our testers. These times are, of course, just for fun, but if you find yourself getting times around the "Expert" time we highly recommend trying your country's National Championships (the US one can be found at **http://wpc.puzzles.com/**).

We look forward to hearing your thoughts, suggestions, and any comments you might have regarding this book. Just e-mail us at **worldsgreatestpuzzles@gmail.com**.

Wei-Hwa Huang
Will Shortz

Acknowledgements

A book like this would be fraught with errors were it not for the hard work of our multiple testers and puzzle-checkers. We'd like to thank the following people for their help in making this book a reality:

Roger Barkan	Dan Katz
Zack Butler	Trisha Lantznester
Joe DeVincentis	Palmer Mebane
Todd Geldon	Thomas Snyder
Isabella Gershtein	Ian Tullis
Tyler Hinman	Jason Zuffranieri

Training
Puzzles

Training Puzzles

The first half of the book is a warm-up to help familiarize yourself with the puzzles. Most of the puzzles in this section are easier puzzles that have been constructed especially for this book, to help you discover some of the basic solving techniques.

If you need help getting started, we've provided Tutorials for some of the puzzle types. The types that have a puzzle with a Tutorial are marked with an asterisk (*) below.

We'll start with a couple of observation puzzles: **Find the Differences** and **3D Maze**. And while we're looking at twisty paths, you'll be introduced to **Loop***, the first of many grid-based puzzles.

The World Puzzle Championship is culture neutral, so the "word" puzzles of **Word Weave**, **Domino Castle***, **Crack it On**, and **Number Spread** either use familiar numbers or don't require you to know what the words mean.

Clouds*, **Honey Islands**, **Ones and Fives**, and **Boomerangs** are shape-placing puzzles, where you place shapes in a grid to satisfy certain constraints.

Nurikabe, **Minesweeper**, and **Tapa*** are "binary" local constraint-satisfaction puzzles, where the clues are sprinkled throughout the grid to help you determine whether a cell is "off" or "on."

We next test your ability to do arithmetic, with **Coins**, **Zero Kakuro**, **Balance**, and **Japanese Sums**. The last one could be considered one of the early sudoku-like imitators, and so ...

... we transition into a set of "Latin Square" puzzles (puzzles where you need to have one of everything in each row and column). You won't find any true sudoku in this book, but we hope **Easy as ABC**, **Ikebana**, and **Missing Skyscrapers** will give you a feel of the range of puzzles that are possible with this design.

And finally, we close off the training session with **Star Battle**, a 2003 invention by Hans Eendebak that is well known to WPC veterans but deserves wider recognition, for its ability to have a wide range of puzzle difficulties.

Enjoy your workout!

Find the Differences

The given pictures differ in several small features. Identify all the differences. Some puzzles may have additional instructions.

Example with 3 differences:

  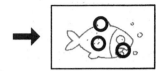

Training Puzzle #1

Par: 16 minutes
Expert time: 8 minutes
Record time: 3 minutes

There are **ten** differences between the two pictures.

Solution, page 160

Find the Differences

(Instructions, page 3)

Puzzle #2

Par: 15 minutes
Expert time: 7 minutes
Record time: 1 minutes

There are **ten** differences between the two pictures.

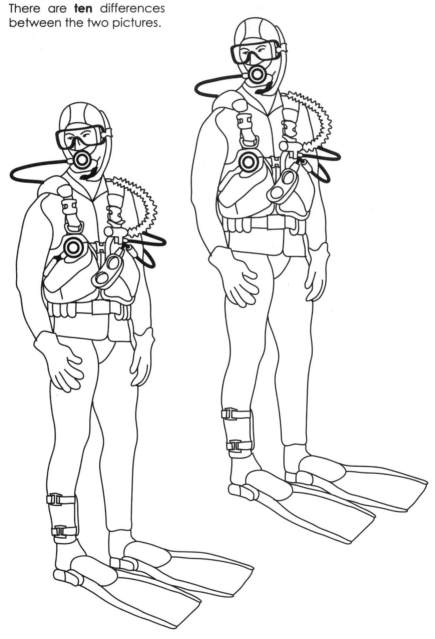

Solution, page 163

3D Maze

Find a path from S to F, through the different levels. Only white cells have a hole in their floor; that is, you may travel straight up or down between two consecutive levels if and only if the cell on the higher level is white.

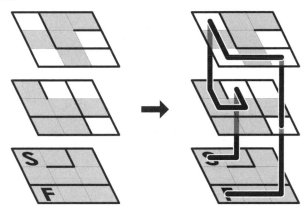

Training Puzzle #1

Par: 20 minutes
Expert time: 6 minutes
Record time: 40 seconds

Solution, page 160

5

3D Maze
(Instructions, page 5)
Puzzle #2

Par: 25 minutes
Expert time: 4 minutes
Record time: 40 seconds

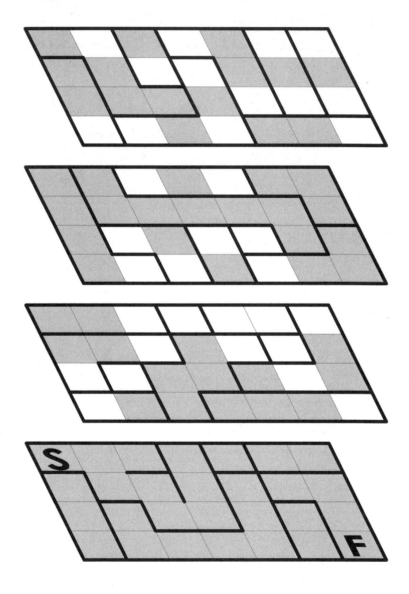

6

Solution, page 163

Loop

Draw a continuous loop through the cells that visits every non-black cell exactly once. The loop must only connect orthogonally adjacent cells (no diagonal connections) and must go straight (not turn) at every cell marked with a white circle.

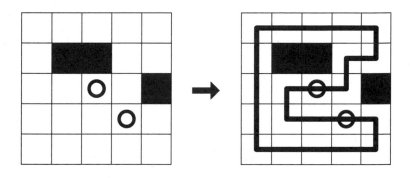

Training Puzzle #1

Par: 2 minutes
Expert time: 1 minutes
Record time: 3 seconds

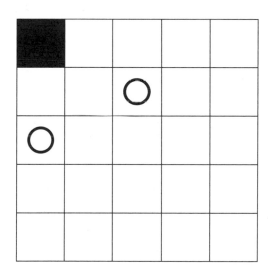

Loop
(Instructions, page 7)

Puzzle #2

Par: 10 minutes
Expert time: 2 minutes
Record time: 10 seconds

A tutorial for this puzzle is on page 194.

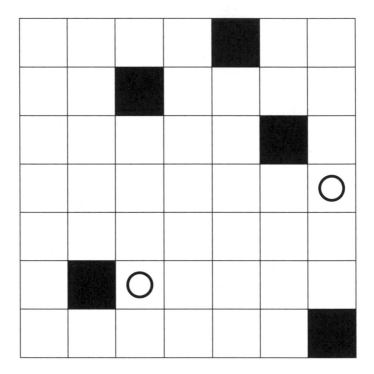

Solution, page 163

Loop
(Instructions, page 7)

Puzzle #3

Par: 7 minutes
Expert time: 1 minutes
Record time: 10 seconds

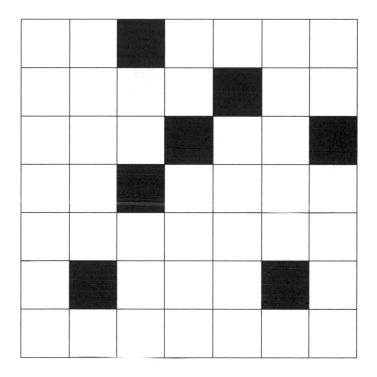

Loop
(Instructions, page 7)

Puzzle #4

Par: 10 minutes
Expert time: 2 minutes
Record time: 26 seconds

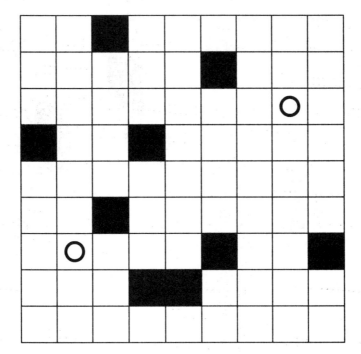

Solution, page 166

Loop
(Instructions, page 7)

Puzzle #5

Par: 11 minutes
Expert time: 2 minutes
Record time: 35 seconds

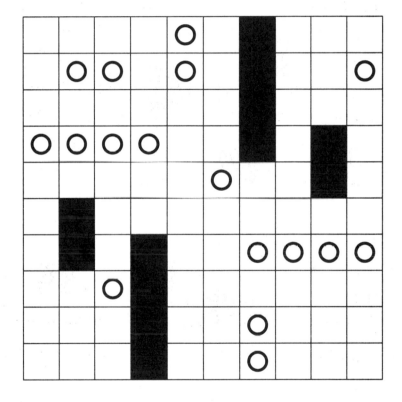

Loop
(Instructions, page 7)

Puzzle #6

Par: 15 minutes
Expert time: 3 minutes
Record time: 40 seconds

A Hint is available on page 198.

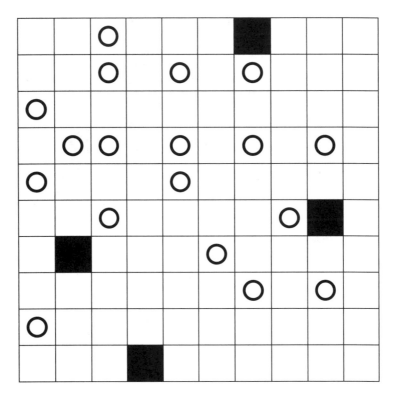

Solution, page 170

Word Weave

The given list of words are hidden in the grid, exactly one word in each row and each column, with each word used exactly once. The letters in each word are not necessarily in the grid in order, or even in adjacent cells. Each letter in the grid is used in *exactly* one word. Identify which word goes in which row or column, as well as which word each letter is part of.

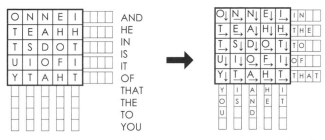

Training Puzzle #1

Par: 14 minutes
Expert time: 6 minutes
Record time: 3 minutes

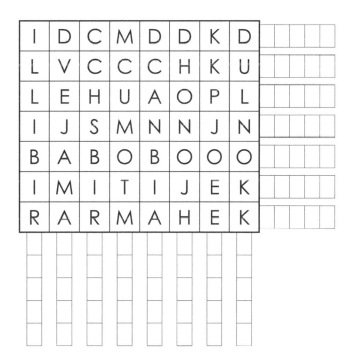

I	D	C	M	D	D	K	D
L	V	C	C	C	H	K	U
L	E	H	U	A	O	P	L
I	J	S	M	N	N	J	N
B	A	B	O	B	O	O	O
I	M	I	T	I	J	E	K
R	A	R	M	A	H	E	K

BILL
BOB
CHRIS
CHUCK
DAN
DAVE
DICK
DON
JIM
JOE
JOHN
MARK
MIKE
PAUL
TOM

Word Weave
(Instructions, page 13)
Puzzle #2

Par: 40 minutes
Expert time: 20 minutes
Record time: 9 minutes

T	O	O	R	O	S	C	R	R	S	E	G
S	G	F	D	R	E	I	I	U	R	O	V
I	M	U	O	E	H	R	O	I	K	Y	L
O	N	L	T	R	G	I	E	S	A	N	R
O	L	A	I	B	S	C	A	A	E	R	O
Q	E	W	U	A	I	A	A	T	S	U	R
R	G	A	T	O	R	N	C	T	A	E	D
P	B	B	G	B	T	R	B	I	A	K	R
H	I	T	S	P	E	I	S	I	E	O	N
S	R	R	E	A	A	O	S	S	N	M	I
R	I	E	R	A	C	P	E	A	E	C	N
C	S	F	U	T	O	U	P	G	R	A	A

RAT
WATERBUFFALO
TIGER
RABBIT
DRAGON
SNAKE
HORSE
SHEEP
MONKEY
ROOSTER
DOG
BOAR

ARIES	LEO	SAGITTARIUS
TAURUS	VIRGO	CAPRICORN
GEMINI	LIBRA	AQUARIUS
CANCER	SCORPIO	PISCES

Solution, page 164

Domino Castle

Place the given set of dominoes into the figure using each domino exactly once. Domino halves touching along an edge must contain the same number. Numbers around the edge indicate *all* the numbers that are used along that row or column, but are not necessarily given in the same order in which the numbers appear.

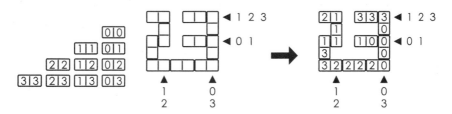

Training Puzzle #1

A tutorial for this puzzle is on page 195.

Par: 35 minutes
Expert time: 14 minutes
Record time: 4 minutes

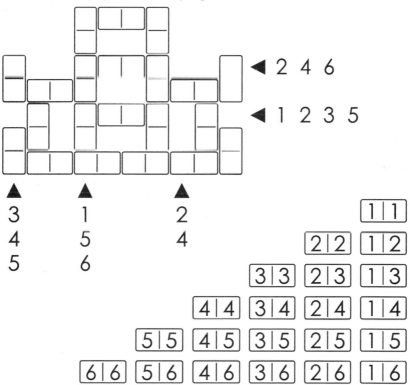

Domino Castle
(Instructions, page 15)
Puzzle #2

Par: 25 minutes
Expert time: 12 minutes
Record time: 2 minutes

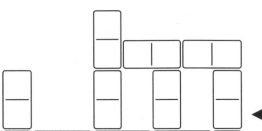

◀ 2 3 4 5

◀ 2 3 5 6

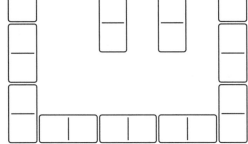

◀ 3 5 6

▲   ▲   ▲
2   1   2
3   5   4
           6   5

		1	1	
		2	2	1	2
	3	3	2	3	1	3
4	4	3	4	2	4	1	4
5	5	4	5	3	5	2	5	1	5
6	6	5	6	4	6	3	6	2	6	1	6

Solution, page 162

Domino Castle
(Instructions, page 15)
Puzzle #4

Par: 54 minutes
Expert time: 25 minutes
Record time: 8 minutes

A Hint is available on page 198.

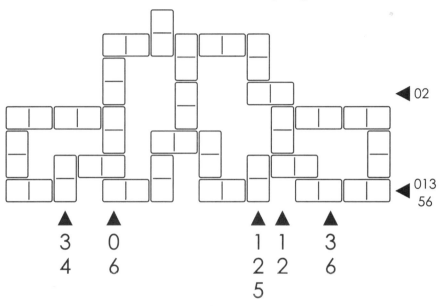

Solution, page 167

Domino Castle
(Instructions, page 15)
Puzzle #4

Par: 54 minutes
Expert time: 25 minutes
Record time: 8 minutes

A Hint is available on page 198.

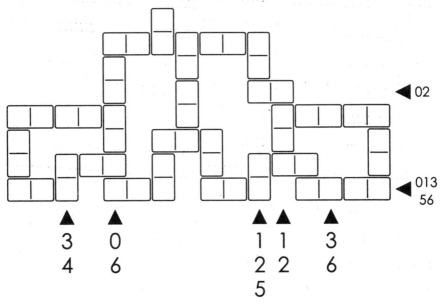

Solution, page 167

Crack It On

Fill in each cell with a single letter such that each "word" in the given list can be read across a horizontal row or down a vertical column in the grid. Certain squares in the grid have been merged together to create large cells that may span multiple rows and/or columns. Harder puzzles have multiple grids that share a common wordlist.

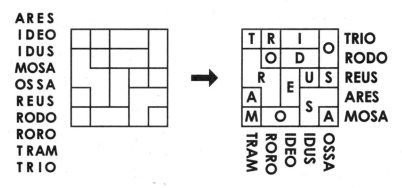

Training Puzzle #1

Par: 8 minutes
Expert time: 2 minutes
Record time: 30 seconds

ASHY
ATES
EHOY
MYST
OYSA
PEAS
PROM
REST
RHEA
STAT

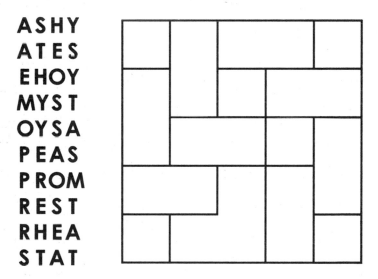

Crack It On

(Instructions, page 19)

Puzzle #2

Par: 8 minutes
Expert time: 3 minutes
Record time: 1 minute

```
AFROS     MITNA
AORTA     MOONS
APSCA     OFAMA
AUROC     ORFUI
FRUIT     OTAMI
ITASA     TROOP
```

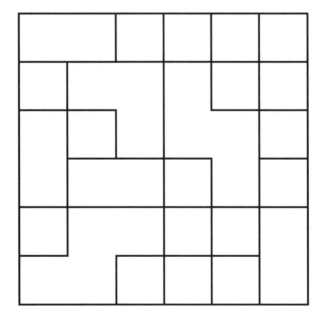

Solution, page 162

Crack It On
(Instructions, page 19)
Puzzle #3

Par: 9 minutes
Expert time: 4 minutes
Record time: 1 minutes

ANT
ARN
AYN
ERE
ERY
FOR
FRY
NEA
NEO
NOR
NTR
OAF
OEN
ONT
ORY
TRY

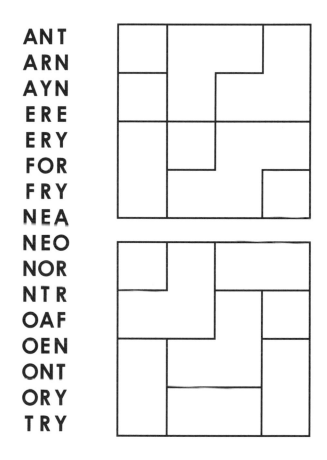

Crack It On
(Instructions, page 19)
Puzzle #4

Par: 9 minutes
Expert time: 6 minutes
Record time: 2 minutes

ATOP
DRIT
EDIT
EPTH
HEST
HORT
IONS
IOTA
IRTH
PIDE
POSE
PUSH
SITH
SNIT
SORI
SPAH
TAIS
THES
TORI
UPOD

Solution, page 166

Number Spread

Write a number in some or all of the six cells. A number can contain any number of digits, and a cell can be left empty. When you are done, the five given numbers should be readable along the two rows (from left-to-right) and three columns (from top-to-bottom).

12, 22, 2213, 22312, 22313

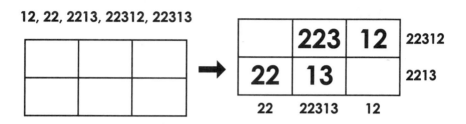

Training Puzzle #1

Par: 4 minutes
Expert time: 2 minutes
Record time: 18 seconds

44, 177, 471, 1474, 7714

Solution, page 172

23

Number Spread
(Instructions, page 23)
Puzzle #2

Par: 7 minutes
Expert time: 3 minutes
Record time: 37 seconds

68, 856, 8386, 8838, 56686

Solution, page 161

Clouds

Place some clouds into the grid. Clouds are in the shape of rectangles and squares, and each cloud is at least two cells wide and at least two cells long. Distinct clouds cannot occupy adjacent cells (including cells that only touch at a corner). The numbers outside the grid, when provided, indicate the total number of cells covered by clouds in that row or column. A cell marked with an × cannot be part of a cloud.

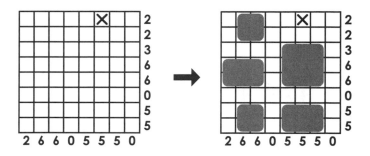

Training Puzzle #1

Par: 9 minutes
Expert time: 2 minutes
Record time: 14 seconds

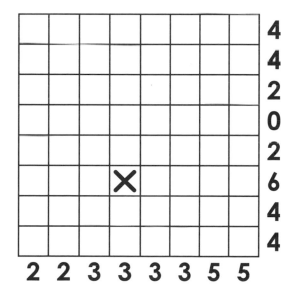

Clouds
(Instructions, page 25)
Puzzle #2

Par: 15 minutes
Expert time: 3 minutes
Record time: 75 seconds

A tutorial for this puzzle is on page 196.

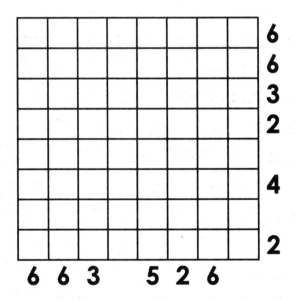

Solution, page 162

Clouds
(Instructions, page 25)

Puzzle #3

Par: 22 minutes
Expert time: 5 minutes
Record time: 67 seconds

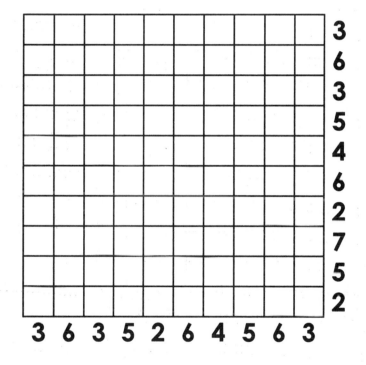

Clouds
(Instructions, page 25)
Puzzle #4

Par: 27 minutes
Expert time: 6 minutes
Record time: 2 minutes

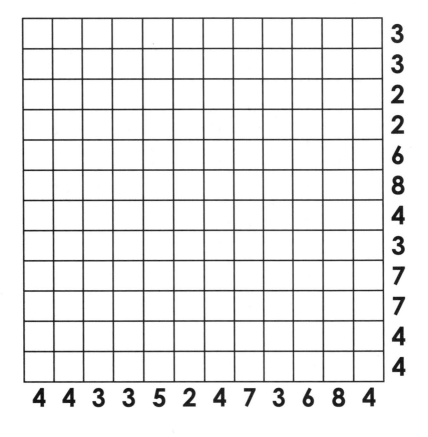

3
3
2
2
6
8
4
3
7
7
4
4

4 4 3 3 5 2 4 7 3 6 8 4

Solution, page 167

Honey Islands

Paint some cells black such that there are six "islands," each composed of exactly six touching white cells. The islands may not touch each other. Some cells are already painted black for you.

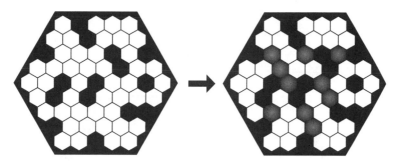

Training Puzzle #1

Par: 6 minutes
Expert time: 2 minutes
Record time: 23 seconds

Solution, page 162

Honey Islands
(Instructions, page 29)
Puzzle #2

Par: 11 minutes
Expert time: 3 minutes
Record time: 45 seconds

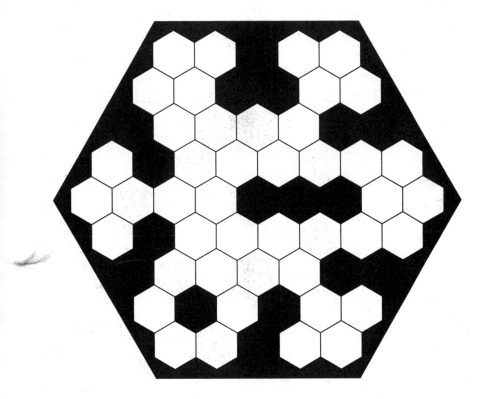

Solution, page 165

Honey Islands
(Instructions, page 29)
Puzzle #3

Par: 11 minutes
Expert time: 3 minutes
Record time: 45 seconds

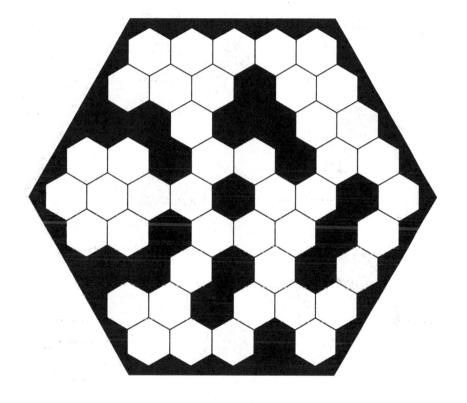

Honey Islands
(Instructions, page 29)
Puzzle #4

Par: 18 minutes
Expert time: 5 minutes
Record time: 31 seconds

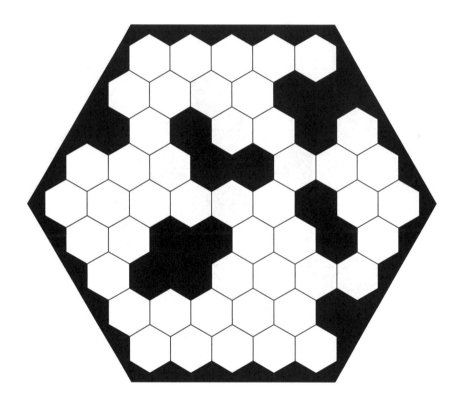

Solution, page 168

Ones and Fives

Draw two "1" shapes and two "5" shapes along the lines in the grid, in exactly the same size and shape as in the example below (which only has one "1" and one "5"). They may be rotated, but they may not be reflected. Shapes cannot touch (even at a corner), overlap, or intersect. When a number is given in a grid cell, it indicates how many edges of that cell are part of any shape.

Training Puzzle #1

Par: 17 minutes
Expert time: 4 minutes
Record time: 13 seconds

Ones and Fives
(Instructions, page 33)

Puzzle #2

Par: 21 minutes
Expert time: 5 minutes
Record time: 22 seconds

		3					
					3		
3	2						
3			3				
						3	

Solution, page 165

Boomerangs

Group the cells into some "boomerangs": two-armed figures that meet at a 120° angle with both arms of the same length. Each boomerang contains exactly one cell with a black dot but cannot contain any gray cells. Each non-gray cell is part of exactly one boomerang.

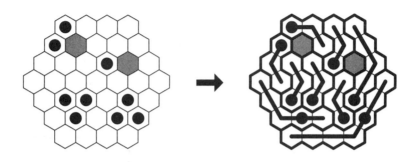

Training Puzzle #1

Par: 4 minutes
Expert time: 1 minutes
Record time: 5 seconds

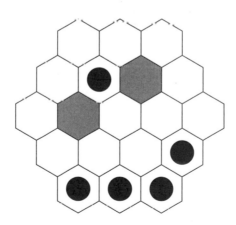

Solution, page 161

Boomerangs
(Instructions, page 35)
Puzzle #2

Par: 15 minutes
Expert time: 4 minutes
Record time: 38 seconds

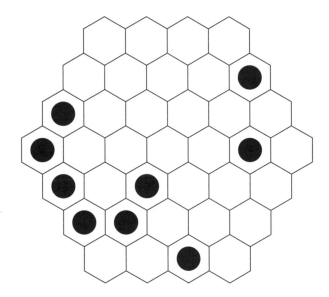

Solution, page 172

Nurikabe

Paint some cells black, representing "ocean," and leave the remaining cells white, representing (parts of) "islands". A group of cells connected orthogonally (but not diagonally) is considered an "island." Each island should contain exactly one numbered cell that describes its area (in cells). All ocean cells must be connected orthogonally (diagonal connections do not count). No 2×2 region can be completely ocean (although it can be completely island).

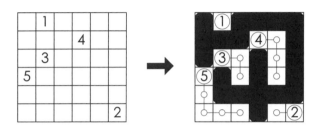

Training Puzzle #1

Par: 18 minutes
Expert time: 2 minutes
Record time: 21 seconds

4							
							2
3							
							2
4							
				5			2
3							
							5

Nurikabe
(Instructions, page 37)
Puzzle #2

Par: 15 minutes
Expert time: 2 minutes
Record time: 36 seconds

A Hint is available on page 198.

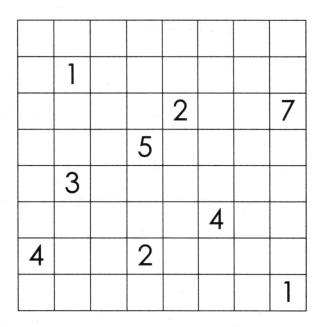

Solution, page 165

Nurikabe
(Instructions, page 37)
Puzzle #3

Par: 10 minutes
Expert time: 2 minutes
Record time: 35 seconds

		3					1	
	1					1		
					1		2	
			8					
	4		1					
		1					1	
	1				4			

Nurikabe
(Instructions, page 37)
Puzzle #4

Par: 25 minutes
Expert time: 4 minutes
Record time: 1 minutes

					2			
2								
						2		
		2	2					
						22		

Solution, page 169

Minesweeper

Locate the mines on the empty cells such that each numbered cell describes the number of mines that cell is adjacent to. Cells are considered adjacent if they share an edge or if they share a corner ("diagonally"). No cell contains more than one mine, and numbered cells never contain mines. You may need to know the total number of mines to locate all of them.

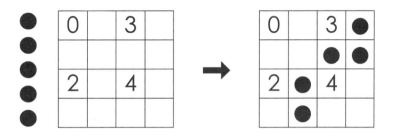

Training Puzzle #1

Par: 6 minutes
Expert time: 1 minutes
Record time: 36 seconds

(18 mines)

		2	1			
	3		3			2
		3		2		
2	2	1			3	
	1		3		5	2
	2		4			
1		2		5		
		1	3			

Minesweeper
(Instructions, page 41)
Puzzle #2

Par: 7 minutes
Expert time: 1 minutes
Record time: 33 seconds

A Hint is available on page 198.

			0			1
	1					
			3	1	2	1
	3					
			4			2
		1			1	
			0			2
2					1	

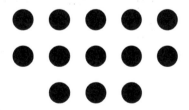

(13 mines)

Solution, page 168

Minesweeper
(Instructions, page 41)
Puzzle #3

Par: 20 minutes
Expert time: 3 minutes
Record time: 89 seconds

1			3			2			
2								4	
3	3		3	5				1	1
		4							
5			5		2				
	4	5		4			1		
1					3		2		
		4		4		2			
				4			1		
1			1				0	0	

(30 mines)

43

Minesweeper
(Instructions, page 41)

Puzzle #4

Par: 30 minutes
Expert time: 10 minutes
Record time: 4 minutes

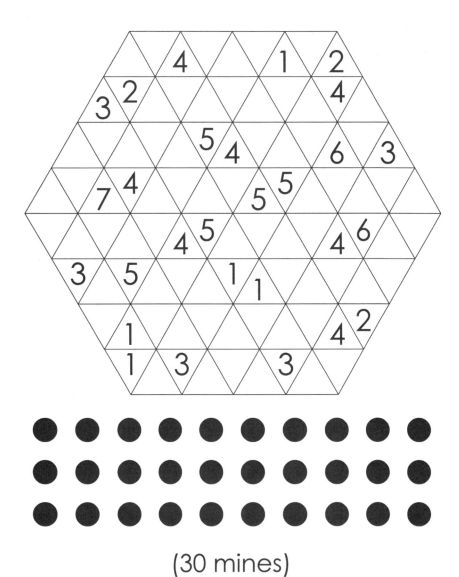

(30 mines)

Solution, page 173

Tapa

Paint some cells black to create one completely continuous wall. Some cells contain one or more numbers; these cells are never part of the wall and their contents indicate the length of wall cell "groups" in the cells adjacent to that cell (including diagonally). Multiple numbers indicate that the group is split by non-wall cells, but the numbers may be given in any order. The wall never contains a 2×2 square.

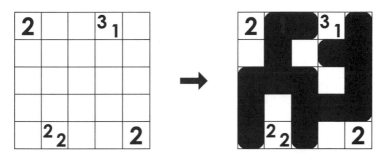

Training Puzzle #1

Par: 17 minutes
Expert time: 7 minutes
Record time: 41 seconds

A tutorial for this puzzle is on page 197.

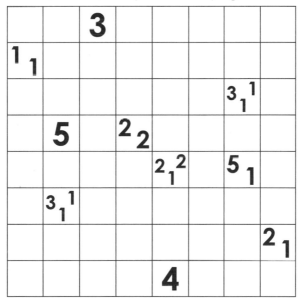

Solution, page 166   45

Tapa
(Instructions, page 45)
Puzzle #2

Par: 14 minutes
Expert time: 3 minutes
Record time: 79 seconds

Solution, page 168

Tapa
(Instructions, page 45)
Puzzle #3

Par: 13 minutes
Expert time: 3 minutes
Record time: 58 seconds

									3
	8			**7**			**6**		
							3		
		5			**4**				
									2 **1**
4									
			2			**1**			
3					**3** **1**				**3**

Tapa
(Instructions, page 45)
Puzzle #4

Par: 18 minutes
Expert time: 5 minutes
Record time: 74 seconds

Solution, page 173

Coins

Place *exactly* one coin into each cell such that the total value of the coins in each row or column are given on the right and bottom sides of the grid, respectively. Possible coin denominations are: dollars (worth 100 cents), half-dollars (worth 50 cents), quarters (worth 25 cents), dimes (worth 10 cents), nickels (worth 5 cents), and pennies (worth 1 cent). There are 100 cents to a dollar. Not all denominations will necessarily be used, and there is no limit on the number of times a denomination might be used.

Training Puzzle #1

Par: 5 minutes
Expert time: 3 minutes
Record time: 90 seconds

$1.35

$1.07

$1.20

$1.30

$2.06 60¢ $1.60 66¢

Coins
(Instructions, page 49)
Puzzle #2

Par: 9 minutes
Expert time: 3 minutes
Record time: 67 seconds

				55¢
				$1.76
				$2.01
				$1.85

$1.51 $2.20 $1.11 $1.35

Solution, page 169

Zero Kakuro

For those familiar with Kakuro (or "Cross Sums") puzzles, this puzzle has the same rules, except that 0 is now a valid digit.

Create a "crossnumber" by filling in each empty cell with a number from 0 to 9. No number can appear more than once in any "word," and the sum of all the numbers in each "word" is provided in the grey triangle on the left (for "across words") or on the top (for "down words").

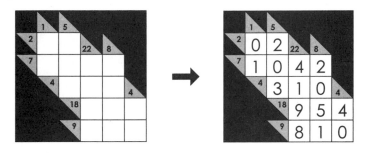

Training Puzzle #1

Par: 17 minutes
Expert time: 3 minutes
Record time: 43 seconds

A Hint is available on page 198.

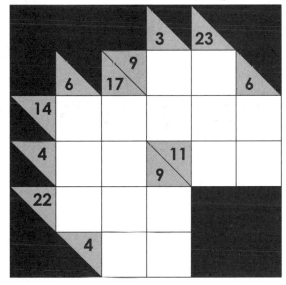

Zero Kakuro
(Instructions, page 51)
Puzzle #2

Par: 30 minutes
Expert time: 9 minutes
Record time: 4 minutes

Solution, page 170

Balance

Attach the given weights (and balloons with negative weights, if given) to the mobile at the diamond-shaped attach points, one at each point, such that the entire mobile balances — that is, at each fulcrum (round black dot), the total torque (weight multiplied by distance from the fulcrum) on both sides of the balance must be the same. (Ignore any weight of the rods themselves.) For some puzzles, a weight (or balloon) is already attached for you.

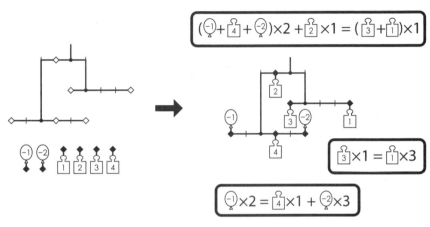

Training Puzzle #1

Par: 6 minutes
Expert time: 1 minutes
Record time: 14 seconds

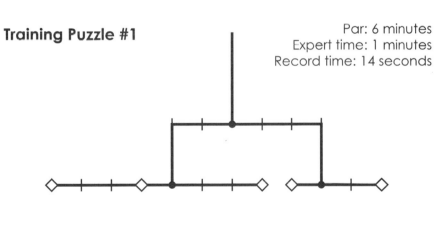

Balance

(Instructions, page 53)

Puzzle #2

Par: 13 minutes
Expert time: 3 minutes
Record time: 75 seconds

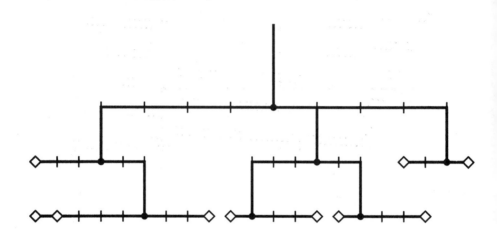

Solution, page 168

Balance
(Instructions, page 53)
Puzzle #3

Par: 16 minutes
Expert time: 5 minutes
Record time: 2 minutes

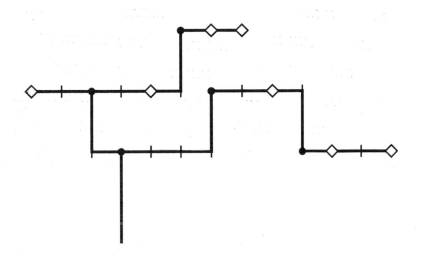

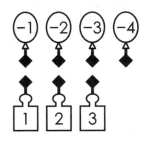

Balance
(Instructions, page 53)

Puzzle #4

Par: 15 minutes
Expert time: 3 minutes
Record time: 41 seconds

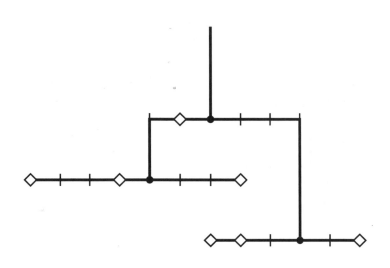

Solution, page 173

Japanese Sums

Place numbers in the given range into the grid (no more than one per cell) such that no number appears more than once in any row or column. A "group" is a sequence of adjacent filled-in cells in a row or column; cells without numbers in them separate "groups." The numbers outside the grid indicate the sums of each of the "groups" in that row or column, in order (left-to-right for rows and top-to-bottom for columns).

Training Puzzle #1

Par: 5 minutes
Expert time: 2 minutes
Record time: 32 seconds

Japanese Sums
(Instructions, page 57)
Puzzle #2

Par: 20 minutes
Expert time: 3 minutes
Record time: 73 seconds

(1~5)

		8	3	13			9
		15	7	10	2	15	6
14	1						
7	8						
1	12						
	15						
8	7						
	15						

Solution, page 171

Japanese Sums
(Instructions, page 57)

Puzzle #3

Par: 8 minutes
Expert time: 2 minutes
Record time: 45 seconds

	6	3			3	5
(1~5)	2	5	4	5	4	4
	4	3	6	9	3	4

8	7						
5	4						
8	4						
2 3	4						
7	3						
6	9						

Japanese Sums
(Instructions, page 57)
Puzzle #4

Par: 22 minutes
Expert time: 4 minutes
Record time: 2 minutes

		5			6			
(1~6)		11	11	15	6	4	6	9
		3	4	5	6	8	11	9
	19							
	20							
	13 4							
5 6 8								
1 3 7								
	17							
7 1 8								

Solution, page 175

Easy as ABC

Using only letters in the given range, fill in the grid so that each letter appears exactly once in each row and column. Cells cannot contain more than one letter, but may be empty (indicated by a center dot). The letters around the grid indicate the first letter visible from that direction along that row or column.

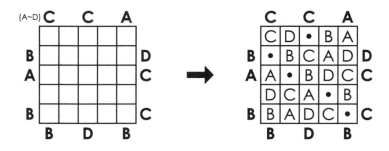

Training Puzzle #1

Par: 2 minutes
Expert time: 1 minutes
Record time: 9 seconds

(A~C)

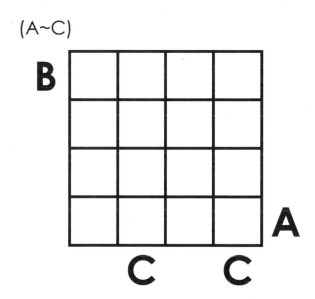

Easy as ABC
(Instructions, page 61)
Puzzle #2

Par: 6 minutes
Expert time: 1 minutes
Record time: 28 seconds

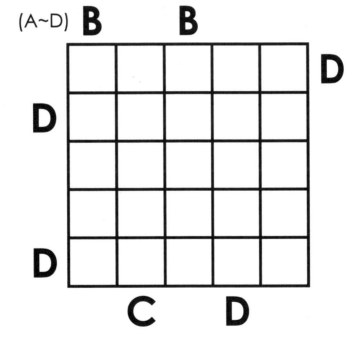

(A~D)

Solution, page 167

Easy as ABC
(Instructions, page 61)
Puzzle #3

Par: 15 minutes
Expert time: 2 minutes
Record time: 32 seconds

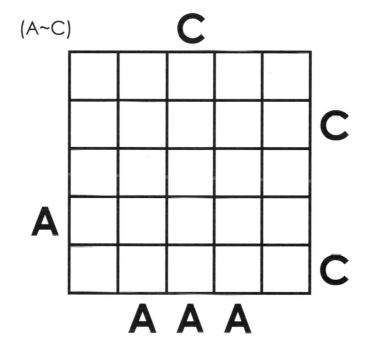

Easy as ABC
(Instructions, page 61)
Puzzle #4

Par: 20 minutes
Expert time: 2 minutes
Record time: 1 minutes

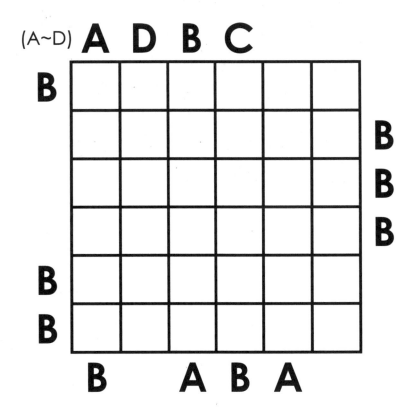

Solution, page 171

Easy as ABC
(Instructions, page 61)
Puzzle #5

Par: 25 minutes
Expert time: 4 minutes
Record time: 2 minutes

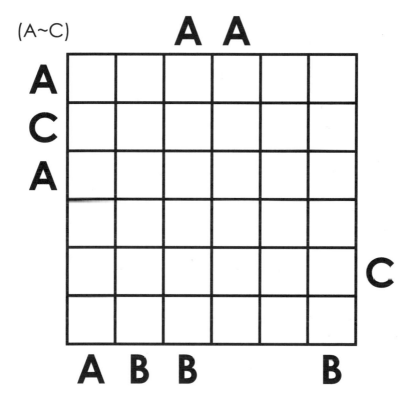

Easy as ABC
(Instructions, page 61)
Puzzle #6

Par: 25 minutes
Expert time: 3 minutes
Record time: 45 seconds

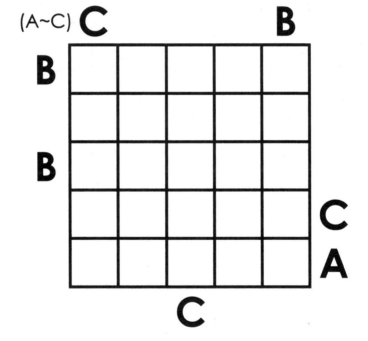

Solution, page 176

Ikebana

Add "black ink" to the cells (but not "white ink"; for example, you could paint a black triangle on top of a small white circle, but you would not be able to put a white triangle on top of a small black circle) such that each of the six symbols appears exactly once in each row and column.

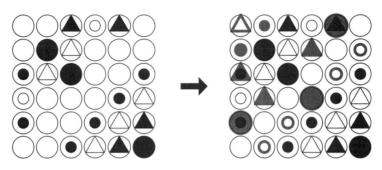

Training Puzzle #1

Par: 8 minutes
Expert time: 5 minutes
Record time: 71 seconds

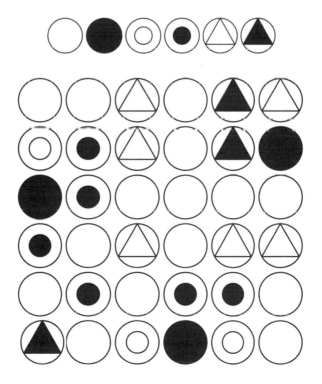

Solution, page 174

Ikebana
(Instructions, page 67)
Puzzle #2

Par: 8 minutes
Expert time: 3 minutes
Record time: 2 minutes

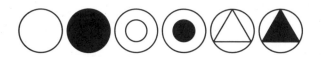

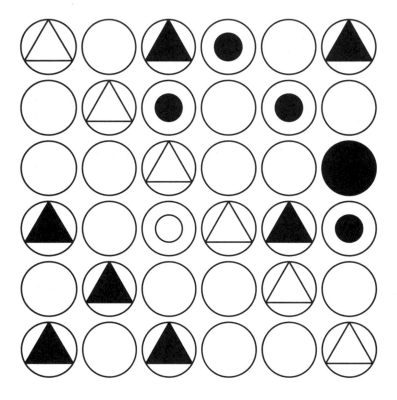

Solution, page 176

Missing Skyscrapers

The grid symbolizes a neighborhood, where each cell is a block that may contain a skyscraper. Each row or column contains exactly one skyscraper of each height in the given range; any remaining blocks are empty (symbolized by •). The numbers outside the grid indicate *how many buildings are visible* along that row or column from that direction, where higher buildings hide lower ones anywhere behind them.

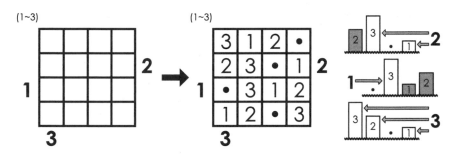

Training Puzzle #1

Par: 6 minutes
Expert time: 1 minutes
Record time: 28 seconds

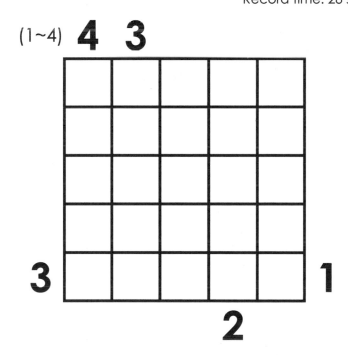

Missing Skyscrapers
(Instructions, page 69)

Puzzle #2

Par: 12 minutes
Expert time: 2 minutes
Record time: 50 seconds

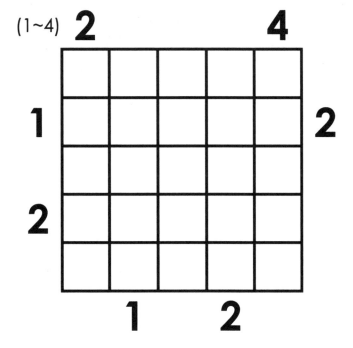

Solution, page 174

Missing Skyscrapers
(Instructions, page 69)
Puzzle #3

Par: 22 minutes
Expert time: 6 minutes
Record time: 3 minutes

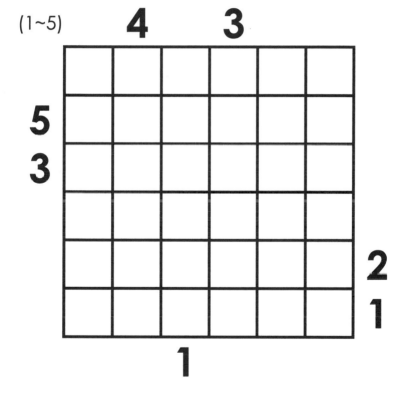

Missing Skyscrapers
(Instructions, page 69)
Puzzle #4

Par: 18 minutes
Expert time: 3 minutes
Record time: 53 seconds

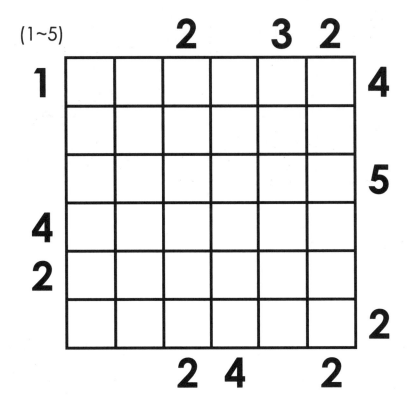

Solution, page 180

Star Battle

Put stars in the grid, no more than one per cell, such that each row, column, and delineated region contains exactly two stars (for the first few puzzles, it will be one star instead of two). Cells with stars cannot touch each other, not even diagonally. Black cells (if any) cannot contain stars.

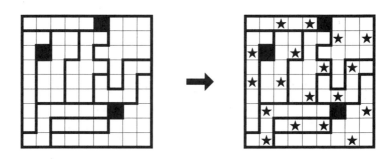

Training Puzzle #1

Par: 1 minutes
Expert time: 20 seconds
Record time: 4 seconds

This puzzle has **one** star in each row, column, and region (instead of two).

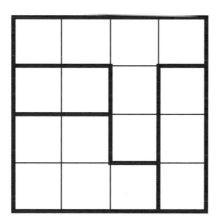

Star Battle
(Instructions, page 73)
Puzzle #2

Par: 2 minutes
Expert time: 30 seconds
Record time: 9 seconds

This puzzle has **one** star in each row, column, and region (instead of two).

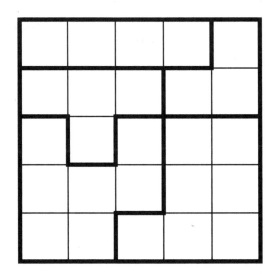

Solution, page 169

Star Battle

(Instructions, page 73)

Puzzle #3

Par: 8 minutes
Expert time: 2 minutes
Record time: 44 seconds

A Hint is available on page 198.

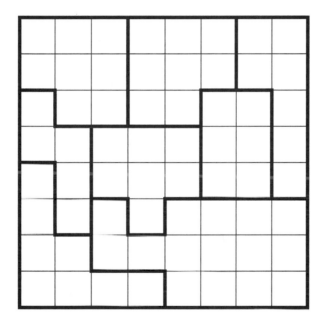

Star Battle
(Instructions, page 73)

Puzzle #4

Par: 5 minutes
Expert time: 2 minutes
Record time: 37 seconds

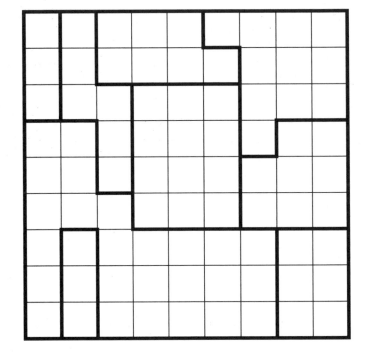

Solution, page 173

Star Battle
(Instructions, page 73)
Puzzle #5

Par: 25 minutes
Expert time: 6 minutes
Record time: 2 minutes

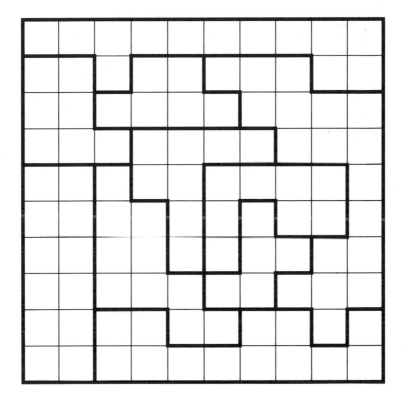

Star Battle
(Instructions, page 73)

Puzzle #6

Par: 80 minutes
Expert time: 20 minutes
Record time: 6 minutes

A Hint is available on page 198.

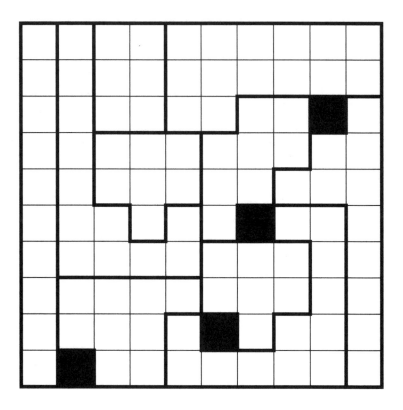

Solution, page 177

National
Puzzles

National Puzzles

Did you enjoy the Training Puzzles? Now let's turn up the heat a bit. This section is half the size of the Training section but will probably take you about the same amount of time to solve (at least, if our testers' times are any indication).

Most of these puzzles are from the World Puzzle Championship, but they'd all be right at home in a nation-wide competition. Just enough to provide a real challenge.

You can work through these puzzles at your leisure, or, if you like, you can set aside a few hours and see how long it takes you to do the whole collection. A time of **4 hours and 32 minutes** or better means that you should consider trying out for your National team. Our best tester, though, managed to finish all of this section in **1 hour and 35 minutes**.

Good luck!

Find the Differences
(Instructions, page 3)

Par: 25 minutes
Expert time: 10 minutes
Record time: 4 minutes

There are **thirteen** differences between the two pictures.

3D Maze
(Instructions, page 5)

Par: 20 minutes
Expert time: 5 minutes
Record time: 2 minutes

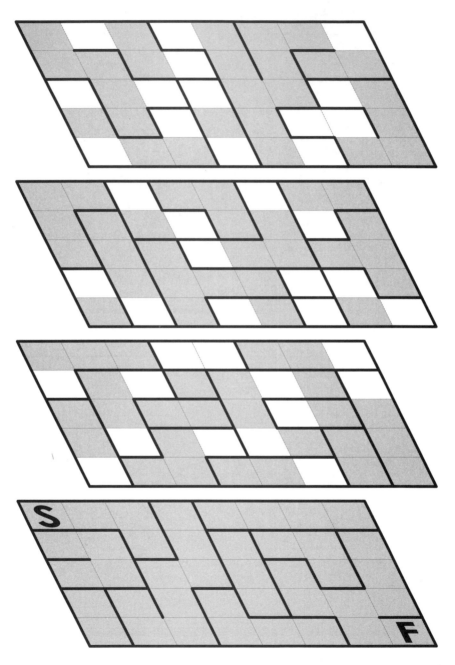

82

Solution, page 172

Loop
(Instructions, page 7)
Puzzle #1

Par: 10 minutes
Expert time: 1 minutes
Record time: 26 seconds

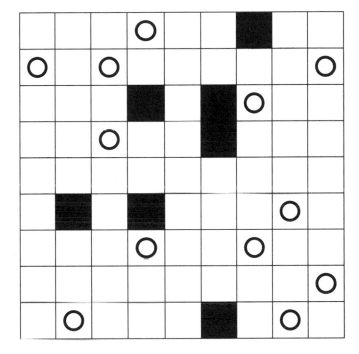

Loop
(Instructions, page 7)

Puzzle #2

Par: 9 minutes
Expert time: 1 minutes
Record time: 19 seconds

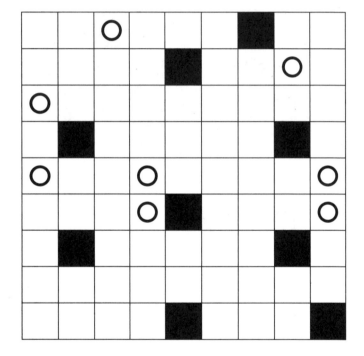

Solution, page 178

Loop
(Instructions, page 7)

Puzzle #3

Par: 13 minutes
Expert time: 4 minutes
Record time: 2 minutes

Word Weave
(Instructions, page 13)

Par: 30 minutes
Expert time: 13 minutes
Record time: 8 minutes

N	K	N	K	U	A	H	A	A
L	I	I	E	L	A	L	N	A
E	A	A	P	U	U	U	P	L
I	W	O	K	W	A	A	K	I
A	I	U	M	L	M	U	I	M
A	H	H	O	A	N	H	O	L
A	I	O	O	A	A	H	U	H
I	I	A	P	L	O	A	P	O
I	K	A	A	U	U	U	K	A

ALOHA	LOA	OHANA
HULA	LUAU	POI
KAHUNA	MAHALO	POKE
KAUAI	MAUI	PUPU
LANAI	MAUNA	WAIKIKI
LEI	OAHU	WIKI

Solution, page 179

Domino Castle
(Instructions, page 15)
Puzzle #1

Par: 25 minutes
Expert time: 10 minutes
Record time: 5 minutes

A Hint is available on page 198.

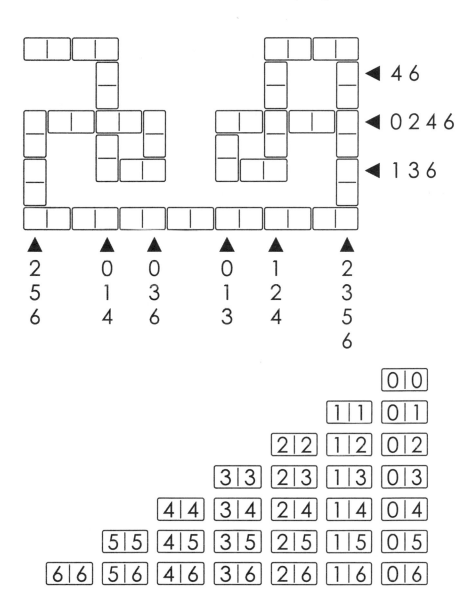

Domino Castle
(Instructions, page 15)
Puzzle #2

Par: 50 minutes
Expert time: 17 minutes
Record time: 4 minutes

A Hint is available on page 199.

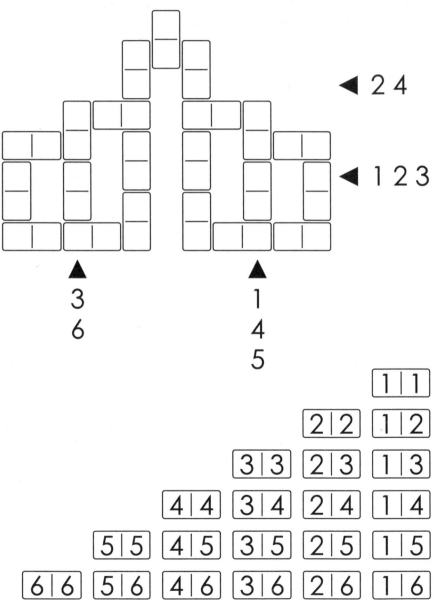

◀ 2 4

◀ 1 2 3

▲
3
6

▲
1
4
5

1	1

2	2		1	2

| 3 | 3 | | 2 | 3 | | 1 | 3 |

| 4 | 4 | | 3 | 4 | | 2 | 4 | | 1 | 4 |

| 5 | 5 | | 4 | 5 | | 3 | 5 | | 2 | 5 | | 1 | 5 |

| 6 | 6 | | 5 | 6 | | 4 | 6 | | 3 | 6 | | 2 | 6 | | 1 | 6 |

Solution, page 178

Crack It On
(Instructions, page 19)
Puzzle #1

Par: 18 minutes
Expert time: 6 minutes
Record time: 3 minutes

APE   HOE   SEP
ESO   HPY   SHA
GAY   HSU   SOY
GYP   IOP   UGH
HAG   PGA   UGO
HAY   POA   UOH
HER   RAH   UPS
HIS   RHO   USH

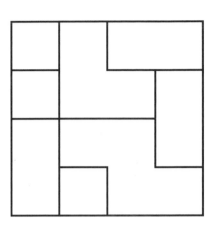

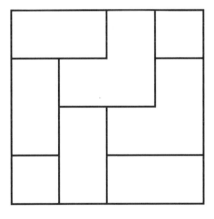

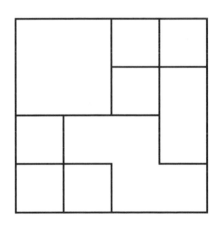

Crack It On
(Instructions, page 19)

Puzzle #2

Par: 23 minutes
Expert time: 8 minutes
Record time: 3 minutes

E E R S E	R E E S E
E R E S E	R E S E T
E R E T E	S E R E R
E S E R E	S T E E R
E S E T E	T E E S E
E T R E E	T R E E S

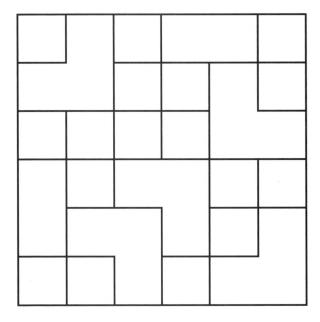

Solution, page 169

Number Spread
(Instructions, page 23)

Par: 16 minutes
Expert time: 4 minutes
Record time: 91 seconds

1, 221, 2221, 11221, 12212

Clouds
(Instructions, page 25)
Puzzle #1

Par: 18 minutes
Expert time: 7 minutes
Record time: 2 minutes

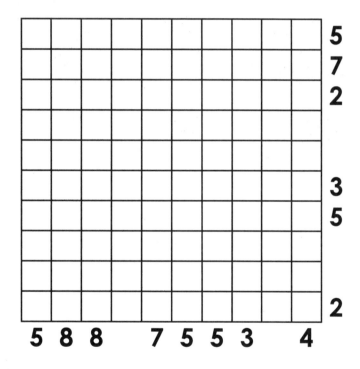

5
7
2

3
5

2

5 8 8   7 5 5 3   4

Solution, page 170

Clouds
(Instructions, page 25)
Puzzle #2

Par: 35 minutes
Expert time: 18 minutes
Record time: 3 minutes

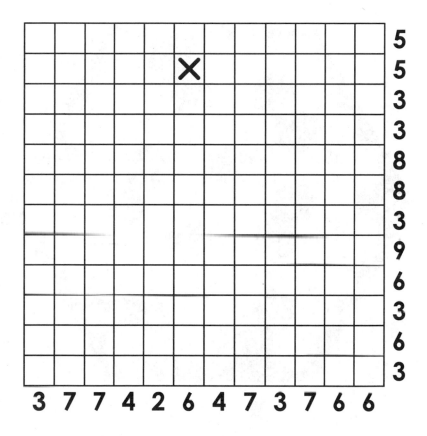

Honey Islands
(Instructions, page 29)
Puzzle #1

Par: 20 minutes
Expert time: 6 minutes
Record time: 13 seconds

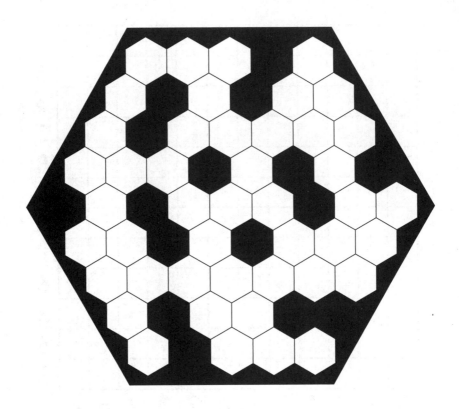

Solution, page 174

Honey Islands
(Instructions, page 29)
Puzzle #2

Par: 26 minutes
Expert time: 15 minutes
Record time: 2 minutes

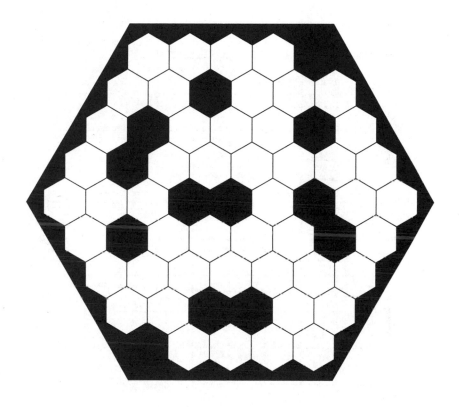

Ones and Fives
(Instructions, page 33)

Par: 16 minutes
Expert time: 7 minutes
Record time: 37 seconds

		2						
		2			0			
		2						
		2						
	2	2	2	2	2	2	2	
		2						
		2						
							0	
		0						

Solution, page 180

Boomerangs
(Instructions, page 35)

Par: 18 minutes
Expert time: 5 minutes
Record time: 44 seconds

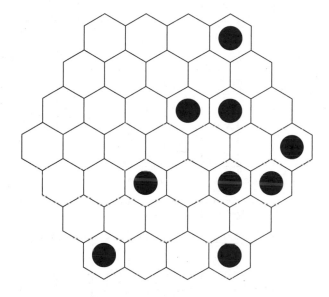

Nurikabe
(Instructions, page 37)
Puzzle #1

Par: 9 minutes
Expert time: 2 minutes
Record time: 36 seconds

			4			4		4
				4				
	1			1				
4			4					
				4				4
	1		4		4			4

Solution, page 176

Nurikabe
(Instructions, page 37)
Puzzle #2

Par: 11 minutes
Expert time: 3 minutes
Record time: 31 seconds

				3					
		9				2			
	2						8		
					9				
		6							
				2			4		
								1	

Minesweeper
(Instructions, page 41)

Puzzle #1

Par: 16 minutes
Expert time: 5 minutes
Record time: 85 seconds

A Hint is available on page 199.

		2				0			
				2	2		2	2	
2				1					
					2		2		2
		1					1		
			2		2				1
				0				2	
	1						2		
							2		2

(13 mines)

Solution, page 183

Minesweeper
(Instructions, page 41)
Puzzle #2

Par: 25 minutes
Expert time: 8 minutes
Record time: 3 minutes

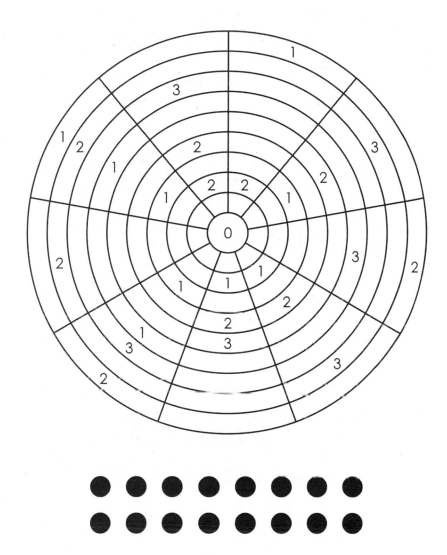

(16 mines)

Tapa
(Instructions, page 45)
Puzzle #1

Par: 18 minutes
Expert time: 4 minutes
Record time: 84 seconds

Solution, page 180

Tapa
(Instructions, page 45)
Puzzle #2

Par: 17 minutes
Expert time: 4 minutes
Record time: 71 seconds

Coins
(Instructions, page 49)

Par: 13 minutes
Expert time: 4 minutes
Record time: 2 minutes

					$1.52
					$2.07
					$1.30
					$2.02
					66¢

$1.60   14¢ $3.75 $1.95   13¢

Solution, page 189

Zero Kakuro

(Instructions, page 51)

Par: 18 minutes
Expert time: 5 minutes
Record time: 2 minutes

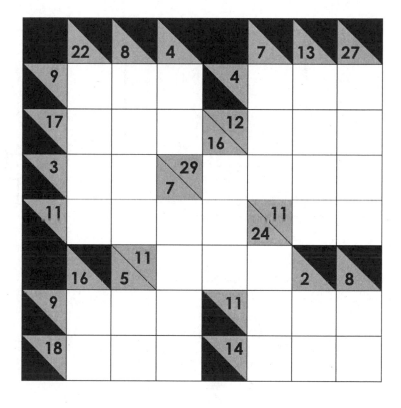

Balance
(Instructions, page 53)
Puzzle #1

Par: 19 minutes
Expert time: 5 minutes
Record time: 78 seconds

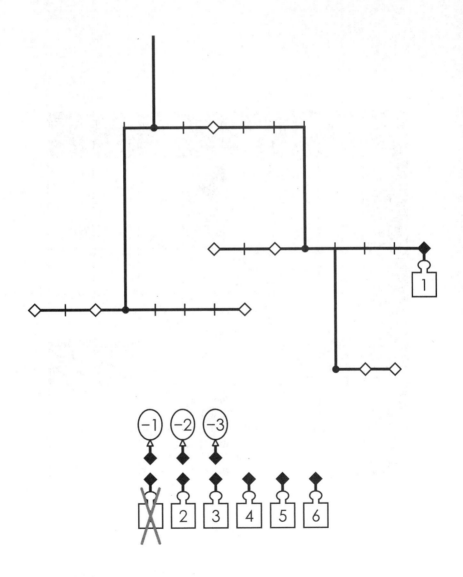

Balance
(Instructions, page 53)

Puzzle #2

Par: 58 minutes
Expert time: 20 minutes
Record time: 3 minutes

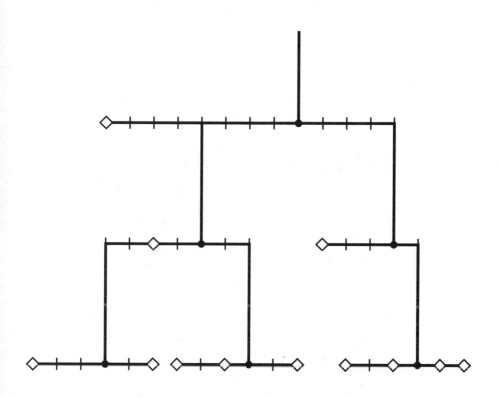

Japanese Sums
(Instructions, page 57)
Puzzle #1

Par: 12 minutes
Expert time: 3 minutes
Record time: 80 seconds

			4			
(1~5)	3	7	6	7	1	
	13	7	7	2	4	14

5 7						
6 5						
3 6 4						
6 9						
5 5						
9 5						

Solution, page 177

Japanese Sums
(Instructions, page 57)
Puzzle #2

Par: 32 minutes
Expert time: 11 minutes
Record time: 5 minutes

				5	10		4		
(1~7)		1	14	6	12	8	12		10
		27	8	1	2	4	5	28	3
7	15								
	28								
10 7	9								
2	8								
5	20								
3 5	8								
8	4								
13 5	3								

Easy as ABC
(Instructions, page 61)
Puzzle #1

Par: 31 minutes
Expert time: 12 minutes
Record time: 4 minutes

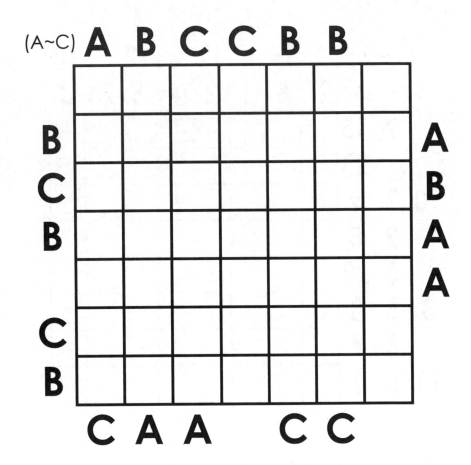

Solution, page 183

Easy as ABC
(Instructions, page 61)
Puzzle #2

Par: 14 minutes
Expert time: 4 minutes
Record time: 46 seconds

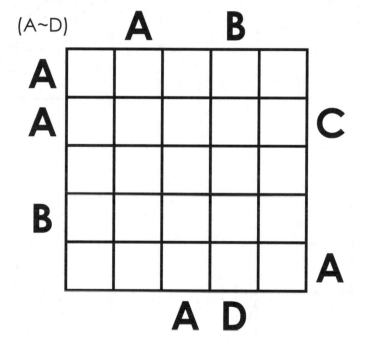

Easy as ABC
(Instructions, page 61)
Puzzle #3

Par: 42 minutes
Expert time: 15 minutes
Record time: 3 minutes

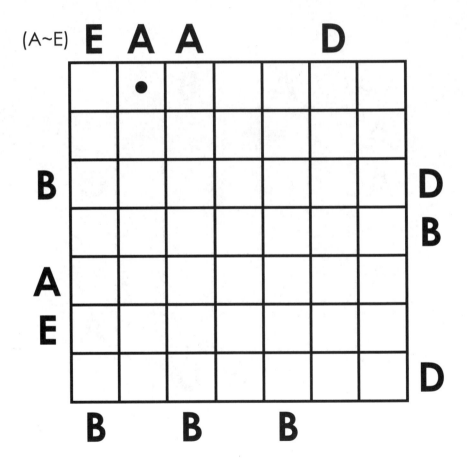

(A~E)

Solution, page 187

Ikebana
(Instructions, page 67)

Par: 12 minutes
Expert time: 5 minutes
Record time: 2 minutes

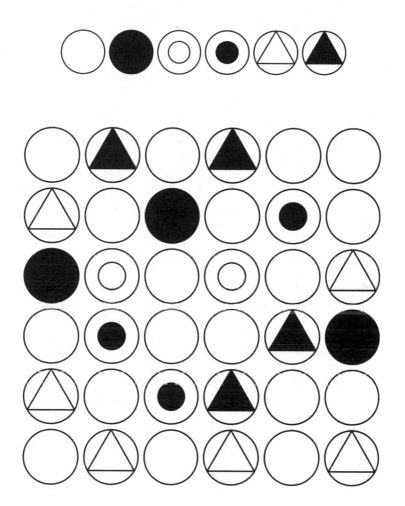

Solution, page 192

Missing Skyscrapers
(Instructions, page 69)
Puzzle #1

Par: 30 minutes
Expert time: 9 minutes
Record time: 2 minutes

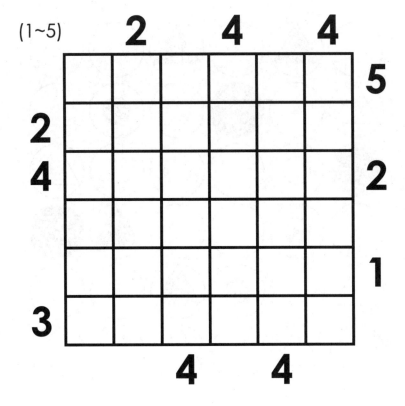

Solution, page 182

Missing Skyscrapers
(Instructions, page 69)
Puzzle #2

Par: 34 minutes
Expert time: 9 minutes
Record time: 3 minutes

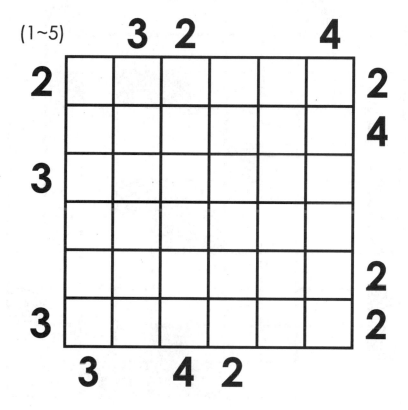

Star Battle
(Instructions, page 73)
Puzzle #1

Par: 20 minutes
Expert time: 8 minutes
Record time: 77 seconds

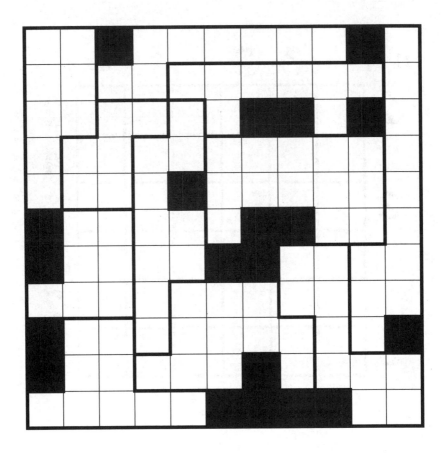

Solution, page 180

Star Battle
(Instructions, page 73)

Puzzle #2

Par: 35 minutes
Expert time: 11 minutes
Record time: 2 minutes

A Hint is available on page 199.

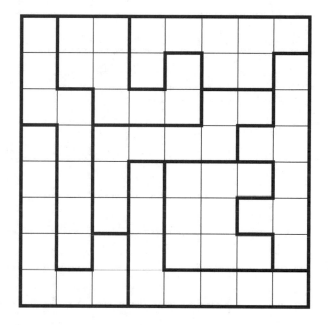

Solution, page 186

Star Battle
(Instructions, page 73)
Puzzle #3

Par: 39 minutes
Expert time: 12 minutes
Record time: 3 minutes

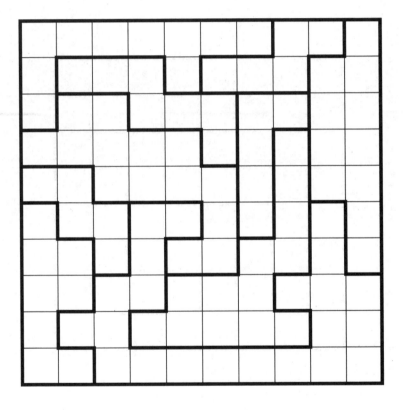

Solution, page 189

World-Class
Puzzles

World-Class Puzzles

And now, the cream of the crop.

Every single puzzle from this group is from an actual WPC, where the rules seem to be "no holds barred"; you'll see some puzzles that exploit the rules in ways you didn't think possible, puzzles that seem impossible to even get started on, and puzzles where even the world's best solvers have to just take a wild guess and hope to get lucky if they're going to finish on time.

Are we scaring you too much? Don't worry, there are also a few puzzles here that are quite managable, just a bit harder than those in the last section.

As in the last section, if you feel up to the challenge, here are the times we've logged from our crack testing squad.

> Expert time: **7 hours, 56 minutes**
> Best time: **3 hours, 55 minutes**

Have fun!

Find the Differences
(Instructions, page 3)

Par: 18 minutes
Expert time: 7 minutes
Record time: 2 minutes

One of the three images is the "original," while the other two are "copies." There are **ten** differences between the original and each copy. Determine which image is the original and find all twenty differences between the original and the two copies.

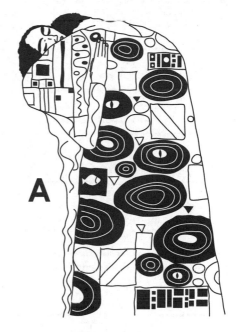

A

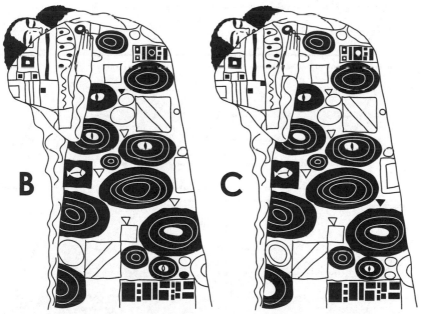

B

C

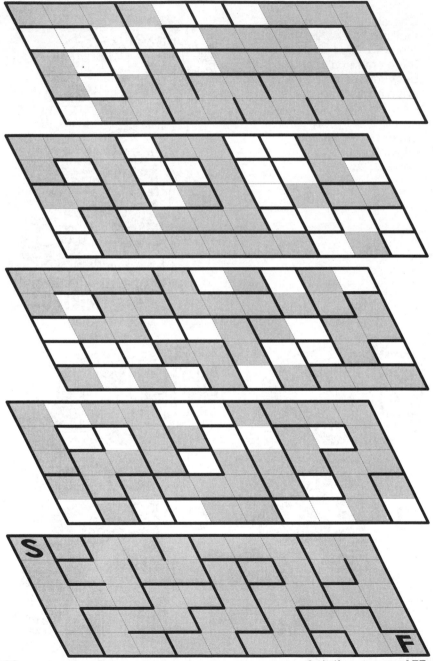

3D Maze
(Instructions, page 5)

Par: 25 minutes
Expert time: 12 minutes
Record time: 5 minutes

Solution, page 177

Loop
(Instructions, page 7)

Puzzle #1

Par: 10 minutes
Expert time: 2 minutes
Record time: 25 seconds

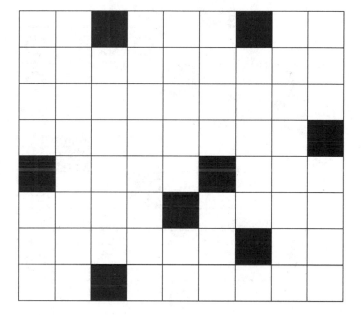

Loop
(Instructions, page 7)
Puzzle #2

Par: 13 minutes
Expert time: 3 minutes
Record time: 51 seconds

Solution, page 184

Loop
(Instructions, page 7)
Puzzle #3

Par: 36 minutes
Expert time: 13 minutes
Record time: 3 minutes

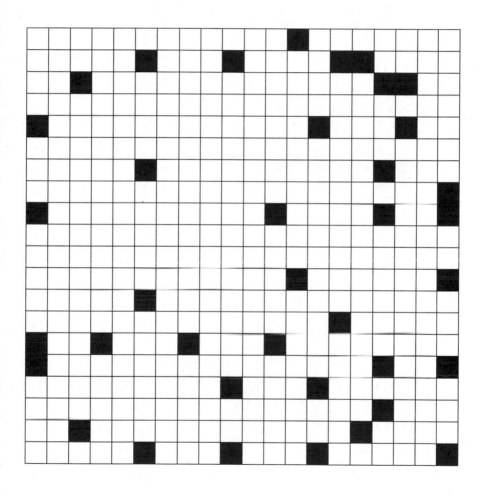

Word Weave
(Instructions, page 13)

Par: 25 minutes
Expert time: 12 minutes
Record time: 6 minutes

A	E	U	I	Z	R	S	B	P	I	L
I	G	R	E	N	A	Y	C	P	R	T
S	A	U	B	R	E	O	A	L	I	D
J	H	I	C	A	C	A	E	A	L	N
A	N	U	H	O	H	C	I	B	A	I
R	F	G	E	N	A	I	A	N	E	I
I	A	A	A	T	I	L	H	Y	G	A
I	C	B	M	G	D	A	N	J	L	L
F	D	A	T	S	N	L	U	A	A	A
M	R	U	I	B	E	I	G	L	B	I

ALGERIA	CHINA	INDIA
ARUBA	CUBA	ITALY
BELARUS	EGYPT	JAPAN
BELGIUM	FIJI	LAOS
BRAZIL	FRANCE	MALI
CHAD	GABON	NIGERIA
CHILE	HAITI	SUDAN

Solution, page 181

Domino Castle
(Instructions, page 15)
Puzzle #1

Par: 73 minutes
Expert time: 23 minutes
Record time: 8 minutes

A Hint is available on page 199.

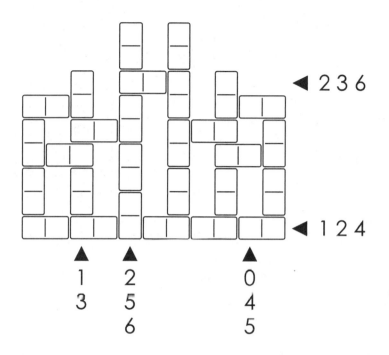

◄ 2 3 6

◄ 1 2 4

▲ 1 3 ▲ 2 5 6 ▲ 0 4 5

0	0
1	1		0	1
2	2		1	2		0	2
3	3		2	3		1	3		0	3
4	4		3	4		2	4		1	4		0	4
5	5		4	5		3	5		2	5		1	5		0	5
6	6		5	6		4	6		3	6		2	6		1	6		0	6

Domino Castle
(Instructions, page 15)
Puzzle #2

Par: 58 minutes
Expert time: 27 minutes
Record time: 13 minutes

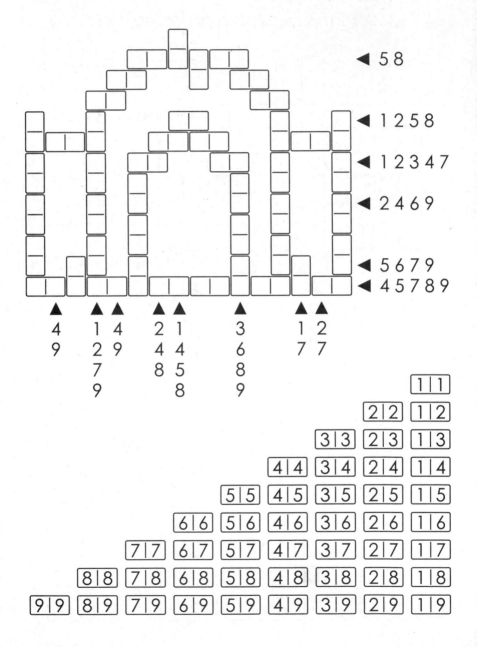

◀ 5 8

◀ 1 2 5 8

◀ 1 2 3 4 7

◀ 2 4 6 9

◀ 5 6 7 9
◀ 4 5 7 8 9

▲ ▲ ▲ ▲ ▲ ▲ ▲ ▲
4 1 4 2 1 3 1 2
9 2 9 4 4 6 7 7
  7   8 5 8
  9   8 9

Solution, page 185

Crack It On
(Instructions, page 19)
Puzzle #1

Par: 20 minutes
Expert time: 8 minutes
Record time: 3 minutes

ANOUS	I RS L F
A S AOL	LAN I S
AU ENO	L FAOL
BA I FO	LORAN
BA I RA	NAOS L
BALAS	NOL I F
B LNUR	NSOL I
BN I BL	R LANA
FARBL	R L FUS
F INRA	RNOEA
I NRAF	ROAFA
I RAOU	U LOAS

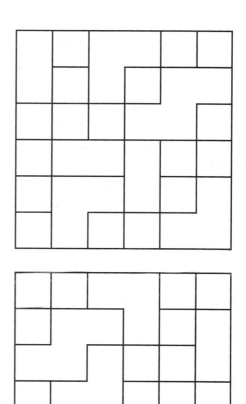

Crack It On
(Instructions, page 19)
Puzzle #2

Par: 26 minutes
Expert time: 9 minutes
Record time: 6 minutes

AGENT	IKADA	OKVIR
AKINI	KAROL	OMORE
AMERI	KASAI	OSRAM
AMINI	KERKI	OTROV
ARMIN	KETME	RAMIZ
AROMA	KORAB	ROVER
ASMIR	KORZI	RTOVI
ATOMI	LIVIA	SARKO
BEARA	MAINZ	SARMA
EMONA	MANAM	SOKAK
EBOLA	MOLAK	TEKMA
GRMAK	NERAD	TREBE

Solution, page 175

Number Spread
(Instructions, page 23)

Par: 4 minutes
Expert time: 1 minutes
Record time: 15 seconds

21, 21, 122, 221, 1212

Clouds
(Instructions, page 25)
Puzzle #1

Par: 28 minutes
Expert time: 10 minutes
Record time: 3 minutes

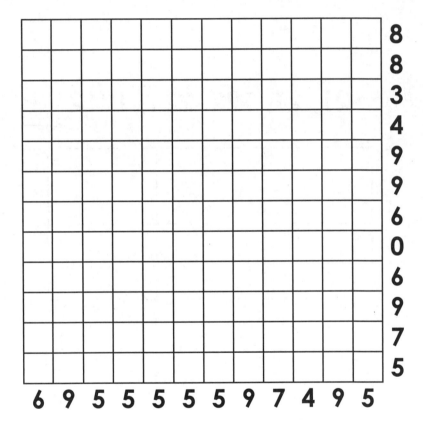

8
8
3
4
9
9
6
0
6
9
7
5

6 9 5 5 5 5 5 9 7 4 9 5

Solution, page 184

Clouds

(Instructions, page 25)

Puzzle #2

Par: 37 minutes
Expert time: 13 minutes
Record time: 5 minutes

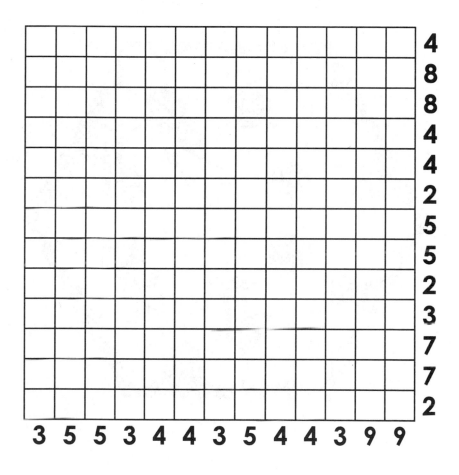

													4
													8
													8
													4
													4
													2
													5
													5
													2
													3
													7
													7
													2
3	5	5	3	4	4	3	5	4	4	3	9	9	

Solution, page 186

Honey Islands
(Instructions, page 29)
Puzzle #1

Par: 10 minutes
Expert time: 3 minutes
Record time: 49 seconds

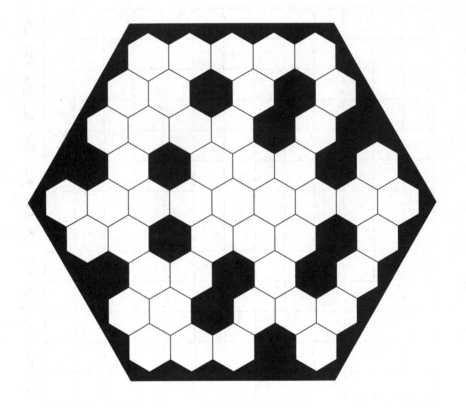

Solution, page 178

Honey Islands
(Instructions, page 29)
Puzzle #2

Par: 31 minutes
Expert time: 9 minutes
Record time: 2 minutes

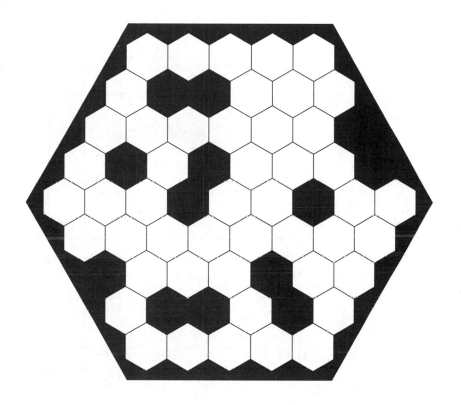

Ones and Fives
(Instructions, page 33)

Par: 6 minutes
Expert time: 2 minutes
Record time: 29 seconds

Solution, page 187

Boomerangs
(Instructions, page 35)

Par: 57 minutes
Expert time: 26 minutes
Record time: 12 minutes

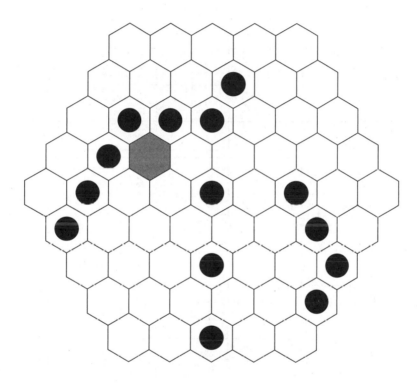

Nurikabe
(Instructions, page 37)
Puzzle #1

Par: 14 minutes
Expert time: 3 minutes
Record time: 87 seconds

2						2	
		2					
2							
					2		
	1	4				4	
				1			
4					4		
			1				
		2					

Solution, page 189

Nurikabe
(Instructions, page 37)
Puzzle #2

Par: 21 minutes
Expert time: 5 minutes
Record time: 53 seconds

							6		
				4					
						2			7
	6								
						6			
			2						
									8
4				5					

Solution, page 191

Minesweeper
(Instructions, page 41)

Par: 51 minutes
Expert time: 26 minutes
Record time: 10 minutes

This is a **two-page puzzle.** Extra instructions are at the top of the next page.

			2				4		
2			3						3
	3				2		4		
					1		4		
			3						
2		3		4		4	2		
			3				3		1
	3								
			3	1	2	3		3	
	1								

● ● ● ● ● ● ● ● ● ●
● ● ● ● ● ● ● ● ● ●
● ● ● ● ● ● ● ● ● ●

(30 mines)

This puzzle has **two separate grids** (on this page and the previous), each containing 30 mines. There is an additional restriction between the grids; no location can have a mine *in both grids*. For example, if the upper-left corner of the left grid has a mine, then the upper-left corner of the right grid cannot have a mine, and vice versa. The thick lines are purely to help you line up the grids and have no significance in the puzzle.

	3	4	3	3			2		
	2			3		4			
							4		
2			2		4				
		3	1						
				1			5		
	2				4	1	3		
	4								
			1		4				

(30 mines)

Tapa
(Instructions, page 45)
Puzzle #1

Par: 15 minutes
Expert time: 5 minutes
Record time: 2 minutes

Solution, page 183

Tapa
(Instructions, page 45)
Puzzle #2

Par: 19 minutes
Expert time: 6 minutes
Record time: 76 seconds

Coins
(Instructions, page 49)

Par: 30 minutes
Expert time: 12 minutes
Record time: 5 minutes

A Hint is available on page 199.

					$1.07
					$1.55
					$1.16
					$3.15
					$1.62
$3.05	62¢	$2.31	55¢	$2.02	

Solution, page 183

Zero Kakuro
(Instructions, page 51)

Par: 47 minutes
Expert time: 20 minutes
Record time: 8 minutes

A Hint is available on page 199.

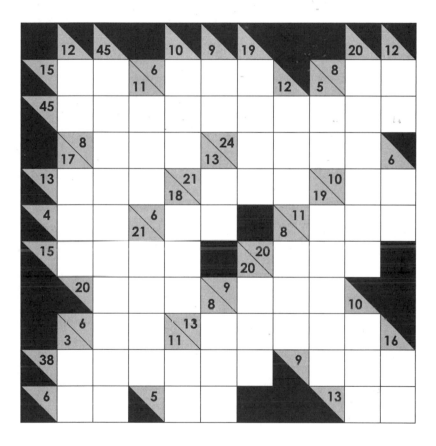

Balance

(Instructions, page 53)

Puzzle #1

Par: 51 minutes
Expert time: 18 minutes
Record time: 7 minutes

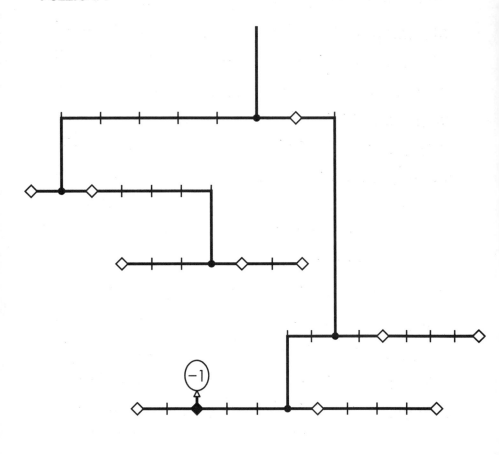

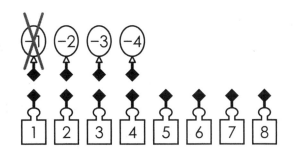

Balance
(Instructions, page 53)
Puzzle #2

Par: 78 minutes
Expert time: 28 minutes
Record time: 13 minutes

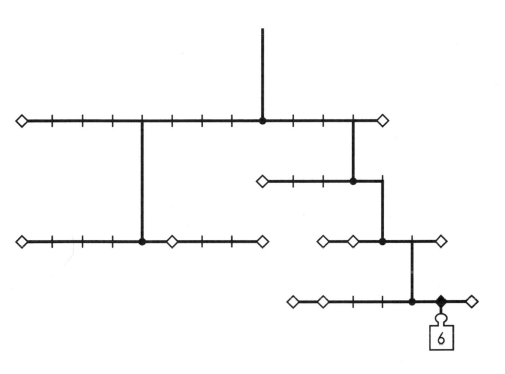

Japanese Sums

(Instructions, page 57)

Puzzle #1

Par: 32 minutes
Expert time: 10 minutes
Record time: 5 minutes

		4				6	17
9	**12**	**11**	**16**	**12**	**4**	**14**	**2**
10	**11**	**8**	**12**	**8**	**13**	**5**	**4**

(1~7)

4 3 13								
25 1								
2 22								
14 14								
7 8 2								
8 9 2								
23								
14 7								

Solution, page 189

Japanese Sums

(Instructions, page 57)

Puzzle #2

Par: 58 minutes
Expert time: 23 minutes
Record time: 13 minutes

(1~9)	6 11 16	25 4 9	4 29	22 21	20 4 19	3 12 11 16	3 27	10 2 20 3	19 19	6 16 20
13 10 19										
13 14 10										
22 5										
22 23										
2 15 4 12										
6 25										
10 20 4										
7 20 17										
5 18 17										
13 20 11										

Solution, page 191

Easy as ABC
(Instructions, page 61)
Puzzle #1

Par: 18 minutes
Expert time: 7 minutes
Record time: 3 minutes

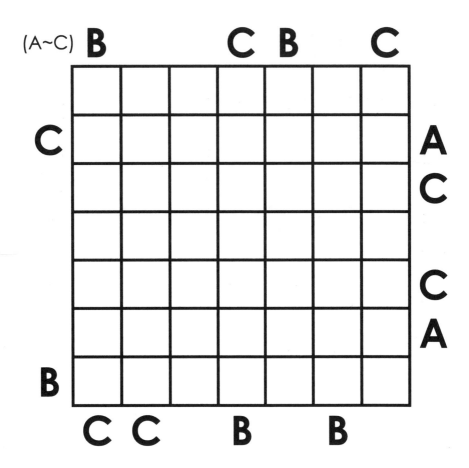

Solution, page 189

Easy as ABC
(Instructions, page 61)
Puzzle #2

Par: 45 minutes
Expert time: 15 minutes
Record time: 3 minutes

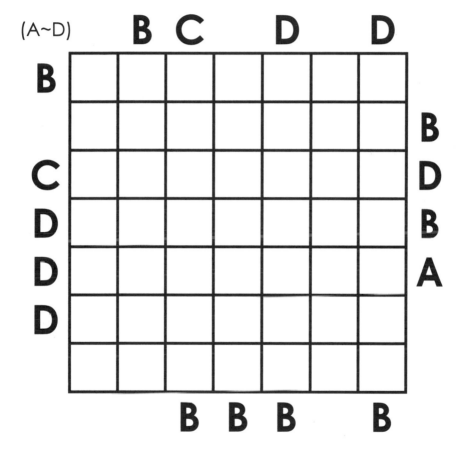

Easy as ABC
(Instructions, page 61)
Puzzle #3

Par: 55 minutes
Expert time: 18 minutes
Record time: 4 minutes

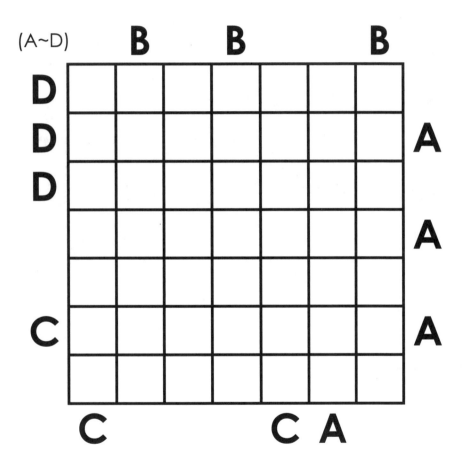

Solution, page 192

Ikebana
(Instructions, page 67)

Par: 23 minutes
Expert time: 6 minutes
Record time: 95 seconds

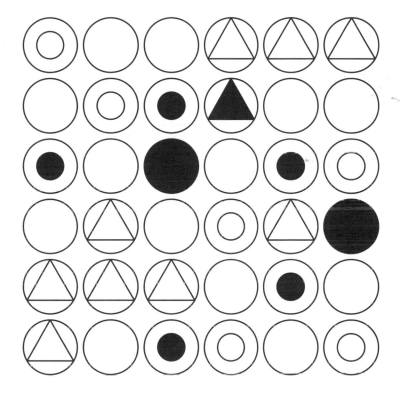

Missing Skyscrapers
(Instructions, page 69)
Puzzle #1

Par: 25 minutes
Expert time: 10 minutes
Record time: 4 minutes

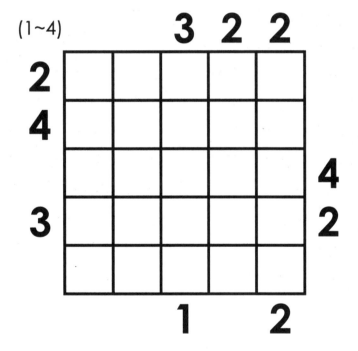

Solution, page 184

Missing Skyscrapers
(Instructions, page 69)
Puzzle #2

Par: 33 minutes
Expert time: 14 minutes
Record time: 3 minutes

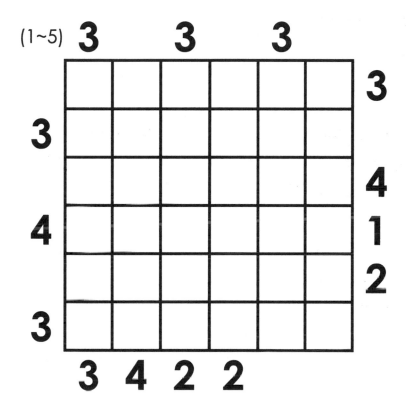

Star Battle
(Instructions, page 73)
Puzzle #1

Par: 48 minutes
Expert time: 13 minutes
Record time: 5 minutes

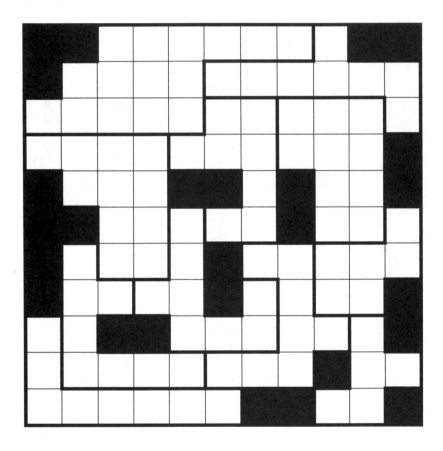

Solution, page 184

Star Battle
(Instructions, page 73)
Puzzle #2

Par: 100 minutes
Expert time: 35 minutes
Record time: 9 minutes

This puzzle has **three** stars in each row, column, and region (instead of two).

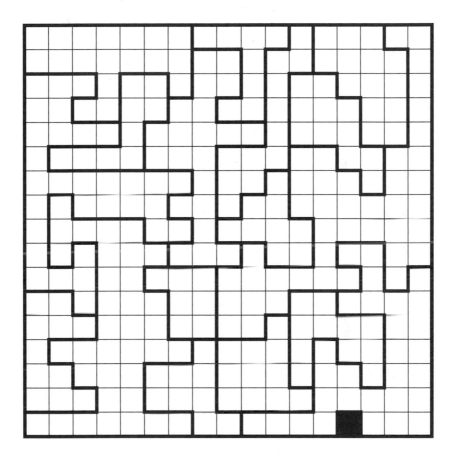

Star Battle
(Instructions, page 73)
Puzzle #3

Par: 130 minutes
Expert time: 22 minutes
Record time: 4 minutes

A Hint is available on page 199?

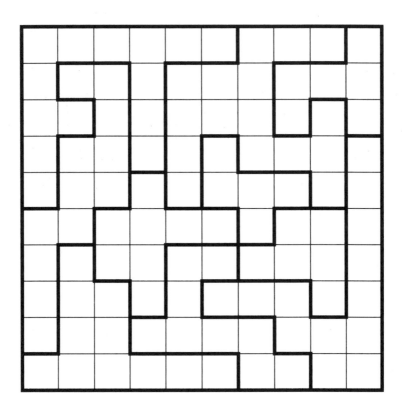

Solution, page 191

Puzzle
Solutions

Each solution lists after it the year and round the puzzle appeared in the World Puzzle Championship as well as its constructor (if known). All puzzles that did not appear in the WPC were especially written for this book by Wei-Hwa Huang.

 3D Maze
Training Puzzle #1

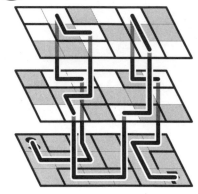

(3) Find the Differences
Training Puzzle #1
2006 Round 7, Bistra Masseva

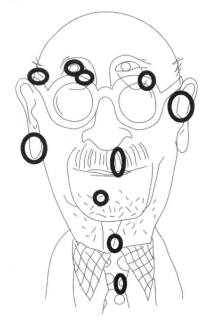

(25) Clouds
Training Puzzle #1

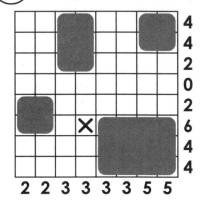

(15) Domino Castle
Training Puzzle #1
2009 Round 3, Atanur Akat

SOLUTIONS

7 Loop
Training Puzzle #1

13 Word Weave
Training Puzzle #1

21 Crack It On
Training Puzzle #3

35 Boomerangs
Training Puzzle #1

51 Zero Kakuro
Training Puzzle #1

53 Balance
Training Puzzle #1

24 Number Spread
Training Puzzle #2
2005 Round 5

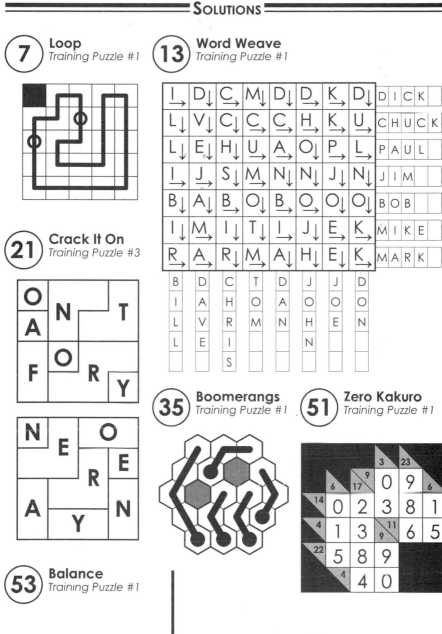

8		838
56	68	6

SOLUTIONS

(16) Domino Castle
Training Puzzle #2

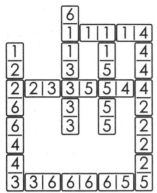

(20) Crack It On
Training Puzzle #2

(29) Honey Islands
Training Puzzle #1

(33) Ones and Fives
Training Puzzle #1

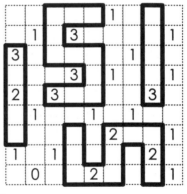

(26) Clouds
Training Puzzle #2
2009 Round 3, Atanur Akat

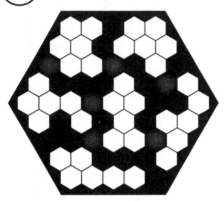

(37) Nurikabe
Training Puzzle #1

(131) Number Spread
World-Class Puzzle
2005 Round 5

1	21	2
22		1

(4) Find the Differences
Training Puzzle #2
2006 Round 2, Bistra Masseva

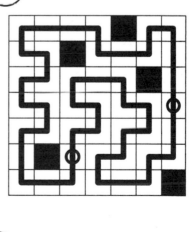

(6) 3D Maze
Training Puzzle #2

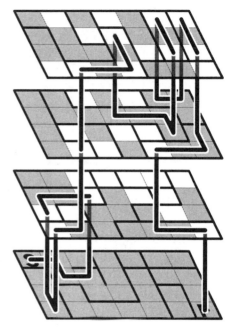

(8) Loop
Training Puzzle #2

163

9 Loop
Training Puzzle #3

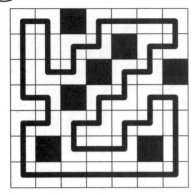

19 Crack It On
Training Puzzle #1

14 Word Weave
Training Puzzle #2

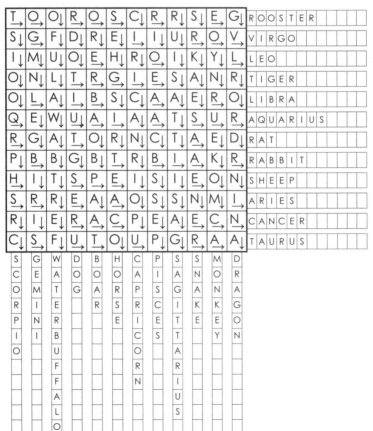

17 Domino Castle
Training Puzzle #3

27 Clouds
Training Puzzle #3

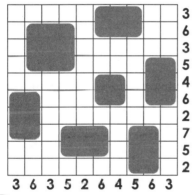

30 Honey Islands
Training Puzzle #2

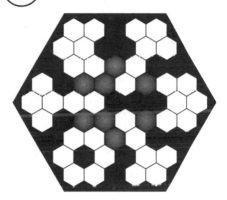

34 Ones and Fives
Training Puzzle #2

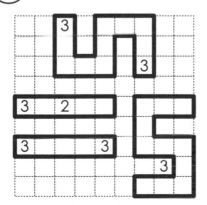

38 Nurikabe
Training Puzzle #2

SOLUTIONS

7 **Loop**
Training Puzzle #1

13 **Word Weave**
Training Puzzle #1

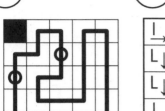

21 **Crack It On**
Training Puzzle #3

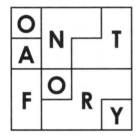

35 **Boomerangs**
Training Puzzle #1

51 **Zero Kakuro**
Training Puzzle #1

53 **Balance**
Training Puzzle #1

24 **Number Spread**
Training Puzzle #2
2005 Round 5

8		838
56	68	6

161

28 **Clouds**
Training Puzzle #4

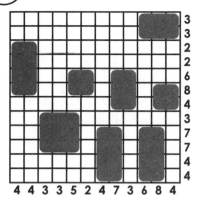

39 **Nurikabe**
Training Puzzle #3

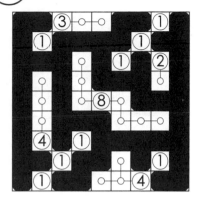

49 **Coins**
Training Puzzle #1

$1	25¢	5¢	5¢	$1.35
1¢	5¢	$1	1¢	$1.07
$1	5¢	5¢	10¢	$1.20
5¢	25¢	50¢	50¢	$1.30

$2.06 60¢ $1.60 66¢

62 **Easy as ABC**
Training Puzzle #2

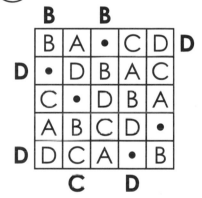

18 **Domino Castle**
Training Puzzle #2

46 Tapa
Training Puzzle #2

32 Honey Islands
Training Puzzle #4

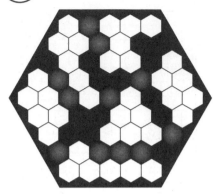

11 Loop
Training Puzzle #5

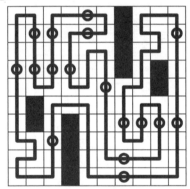

42 Minesweeper
Training Puzzle #2
2004 Round 1

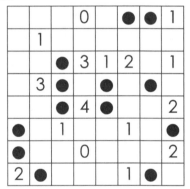

54 Balance
Training Puzzle #2

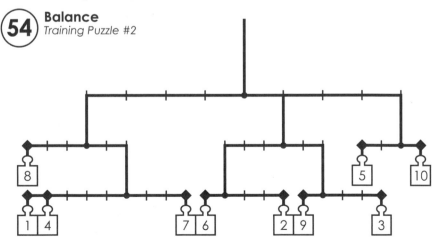

50 Coins
Training Puzzle #2
2005 Round 5

57 Japanese Sums
Training Puzzle #1

40 Nurikabe
Training Puzzle #4

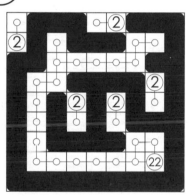

74 Star Battle
Training Puzzle #2

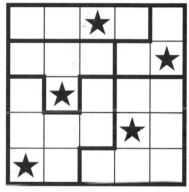

63 Easy as ABC
Training Puzzle #3

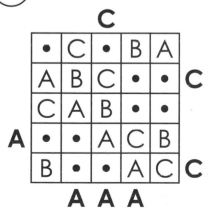

90 Crack It On
National Puzzle #2

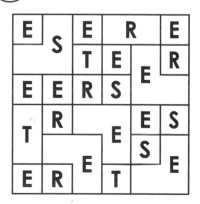

43 Minesweeper
Training Puzzle #3

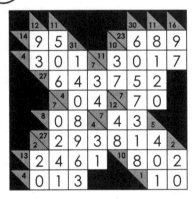

47 Tapa
Training Puzzle #3

52 Zero Kakuro
Training Puzzle #2

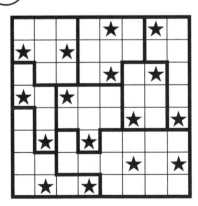

12 Loop
Training Puzzle #6
2004 Round 1

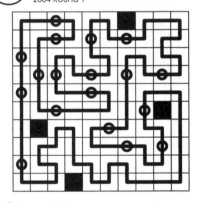

75 Star Battle
Training Puzzle #3

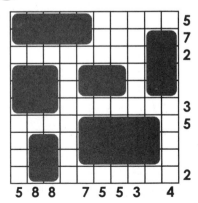

92 Clouds
National Puzzle #1
2009 Round 3, Atanur Akat

55 Balance
Training Puzzle #3
2005 Round 5

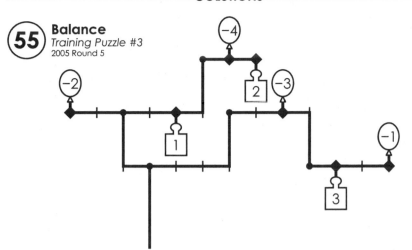

58 Japanese Sums
Training Puzzle #2

$(1\sim5)$

		8	**3**	**13**		**9**	
		15	**7**	**10**	**2**	**15**	**6**
14	**1**	2	5	3	4	■	1
7	**8**	4	3	■	1	2	5
1	**12**	1	■	■	5	4	3
	15	5	2	4	3	1	■
8	**7**	3	4	1	■	5	2
	15	■	1	5	2	3	4

64 Easy as ABC
Training Puzzle #4
2007 Round 4, Ricardo Daniel Kossatz

	A	**D**	**B**	**C**			
B	•	•	B	C	D	A	
	A	•	•	D	C	B	**B**
	C	D	•	A	B	•	**B**
	D	A	C	B	•	•	**B**
B	•	B	D	•	A	C	
B	B	C	A	•	•	D	
	B		**A**	**B**	**A**		

87 Domino Castle
National Puzzle #1
2009 Round 3, Hasan Yurtoğlu

2	5	5	4							4	3	3	6
			4							4			6
			4							2			2
6	6	4	4	0	0			0	2	2	2	2	2
6			4		6			0		1			3
6			1	1	6			1	1	1			3
5													5
5	0	0	0	0	3	3	3	3	1	1	5	5	5

(73) Star Battle
Training Puzzle #1

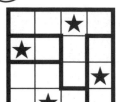

(82) 3D Maze
National Puzzle

(129) Crack It On
World-Class Puzzle #1
2003 Round 1

(36) Boomerangs
Training Puzzle #2

(61) Easy as ABC
Training Puzzle #1

(23) Number Spread
Training Puzzle #1
2005 Round 5

1	47	4
77	1	4

44 **Minesweeper**
Training Puzzle #4

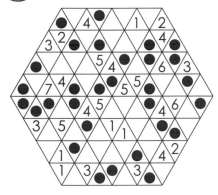

48 **Tapa**
Training Puzzle #4

76 **Star Battle**
Training Puzzle #4

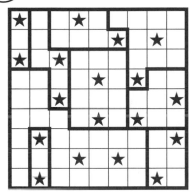

59 **Japanese Sums**
Training Puzzle #3

56 **Balance**
Training Puzzle #4

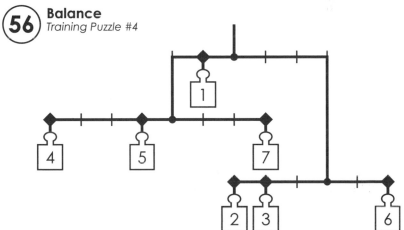

67 Ikebana
Training Puzzle #1

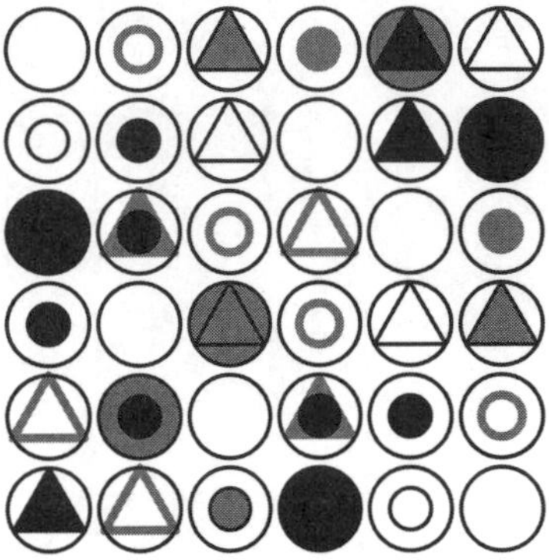

70 Missing Skyscrapers
Training Puzzle #2
2006 Round 6, Deyan Razsadov

(1~4)	2				4	
	3	2	4	•	1	
1	4	1	2	3	•	2
	•	3	1	4	2	
2	2	4	•	1	3	
	1	•	3	2	4	
		1		2		

83 Loop
National Puzzle #1
2009 Round 12, Serkan Yürekli

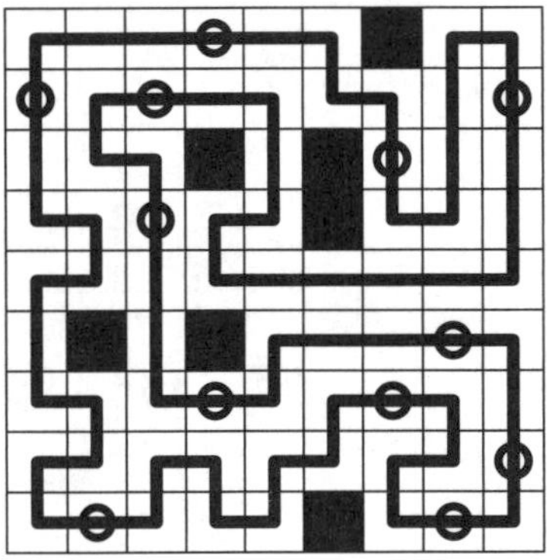

94 Honey Islands
National Puzzle #1
2005 Round 7

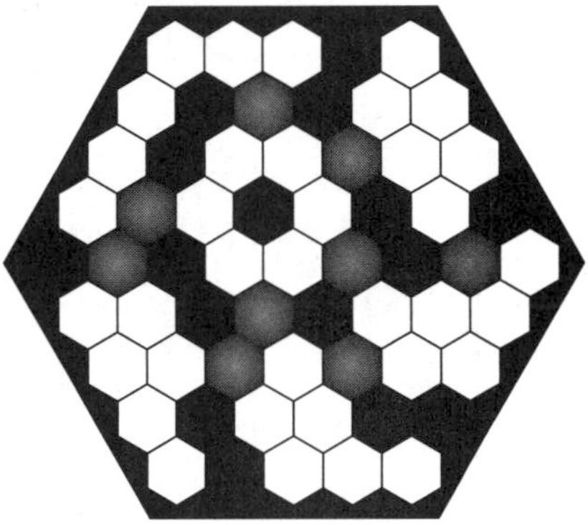

81 Find the Differences
National Puzzle
2004 Round 4

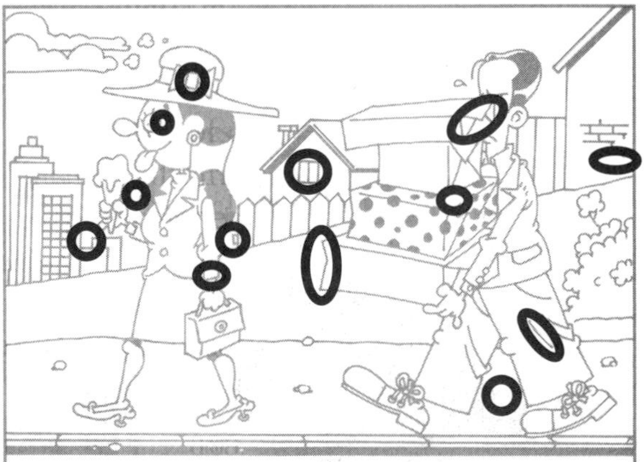

(77) Star Battle
Training Puzzle #5

(130) Crack It On
World-Class Puzzle #2
2004 Round 2

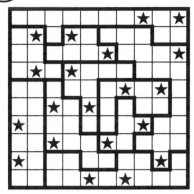

(60) Japanese Sums
Training Puzzle #4

(65) Easy as ABC
Training Puzzle #5
2008 Round 2, A. Fabris, A. Bogdanov

(A~C)

	A	A			
A	•	•	•	A	B	C
C	C	•	•	B	•	A
A	•	A	•	•	C	B
	B	C	A	•	•	•
	A	B	C	•	•	•	C
	•	•	B	C	A	•

A B B B

SOLUTIONS

66 Easy as ABC
Training Puzzle #6
2008 Round 2, A. Fabris, A. Bogdanov

	C			B	
B	•	B	A	C	•
	C	A	•	•	B
B	B	C	•	A	•
	A	•	B	•	C	C
	•	•	C	B	A	A
		C			

68 Ikebana
Training Puzzle #2

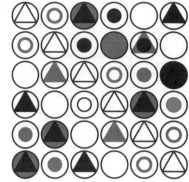

69 Missing Skyscrapers
Training Puzzle #1
2007 Round 1, Daniel Martin

(1~4) **4 3**

1	2	4	3	•	
2	3	•	4	1	
3	4	1	•	2	
4	•	2	1	3	
•	1	3	2	4	**1**

3 (left)   **2** (bottom)

137 Boomerangs
World-Class Puzzle
2008 Round 8, Vladimir Portugalov

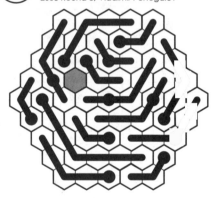

98 Nurikabe
National Puzzle #1

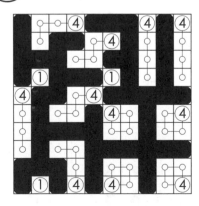

95 Honey Islands
National Puzzle #2
2005 Round 7

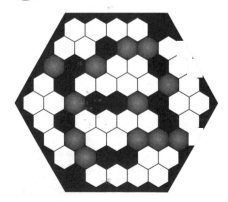

108 Japanese Sums
National Puzzle #2
2005 Round 11

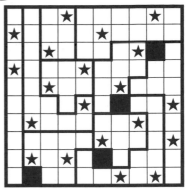

(1~5)

			4			
	3	7	6	7	1	
	13	7	7	2	4	14
5 7	5	■		4	2	1
6 5	1	3	2	■	5	■
3 6 4	3	■	5	1		4
6 9	4	2		5	1	3
5 5	■	1	4	■	3	2
9 5	■	4	3	2	■	5

78 Star Battle
Training Puzzle #6

122 3D Maze
World-Class Puzzle
2007 Part 13, Ricardo Daniel Kossatz

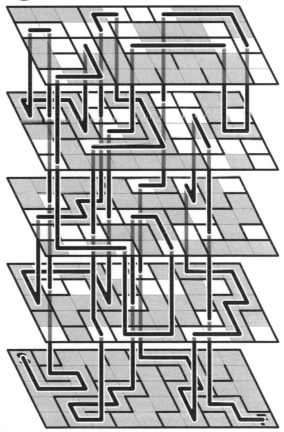

177

88 Domino Castle
National Puzzle #2
2008 Finals, A. Bogdanov

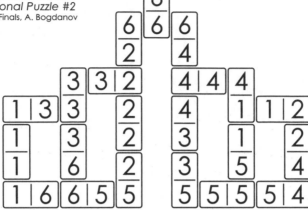

84 Loop
National Puzzle #2
2009 Round 12, Serkan Yürekli

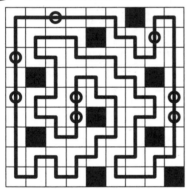

99 Nurikabe
National Puzzle #2

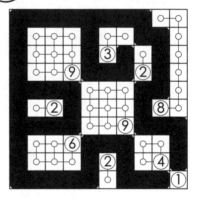

72 Missing Skyscrapers
Training Puzzle #4
2006 Round 6, Deyan Razsadov

(1~5)

	2		**3**	**2**		
1	•	5	4	3	1	2	**4**
	2	3	1	5	4	•
	5	4	3	•	2	1	**5**
4	1	2	•	4	3	5
2	4	1	5	2	•	3
	3	•	2	1	5	4	**2**

2 **4** **2**

134 Honey Islands
World-Class Puzzle #1
2005 Round 7

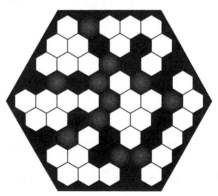

(121) Find the Differences
World-Class Puzzle
2006 Finals, Bistra Masseva

Image B is the original.

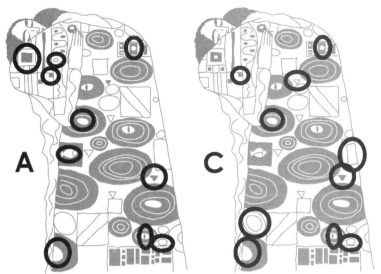

A

C

(86) Word Weave
National Puzzle

N→	K↓	N↓	K→	U→	A→	H→	A→	A↓	K A H U N A
L↓	I↓	I→	E↓	L→	A→	L↓	N,	A→	L A N A I
E↓	A↓	A↓	P,	U↓	U→	U→	P→	L↓	P U P U
I→	W↓	O↓	K↓	W→	A↓	A↓	K→	I→	W I K I
A→	I→	U→	M↓	L↓	M↓	U↓	I↓	M↓	M A U I
A→	H→	H↓	O→	A→	N↓	H↓	O↓	L→	A L O H A
A→	I↓	O→	O↓	A↓	A↓	H→	U→	H↓	O A H U
I↓	I↓	A↓	P↓	L→	O→	A→	P↓	O↓	L O A
I→	K↓	A→	A→	U↓	U↓	U→	K→	A↓	K A U A I

L	W	O	P	L	M	H	P	M
E	A	H	O	U	A	U	O	A
I	I	A	K	A	U	L	I	H
	K	N	E	U	N	A		A
	I	A		U	A			L
	K							O
	I							

179

(85) Loop
National Puzzle #3

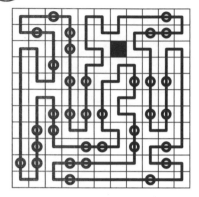

(116) Star Battle
National Puzzle #1
2003 Round 3

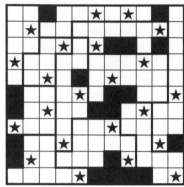

(102) Tapa
National Puzzle #1
2010 Round 8

(96) Ones and Fives
National Puzzle

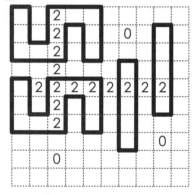

(135) Honey Islands
World-Class Puzzle #2
2006 Semi-finals, Laszlo Mero

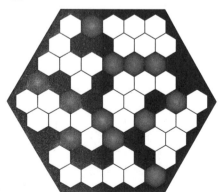

(71) Missing Skyscrapers
Training Puzzle #3
2007 Round 1, Daniel Martin

(1~5)

		4		**3**		
	5	1	2	3	•	4
5	1	2	3	4	5	•
3	•	3	4	5	2	1
	3	5	1	•	4	2
	4	•	5	2	1	3	**2**
	2	4	•	1	3	5	**1**
				1		

SOLUTIONS

(126) Word Weave
World-Class Puzzle
2003 Round 8

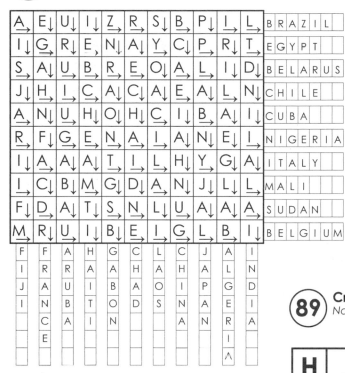

(91) Number Spread
National Puzzle
2005 Round 5

1	1221	
	2	221

(89) Crack It On
National Puzzle #1

181

93 Clouds
National Puzzle #2
2003 Round 2

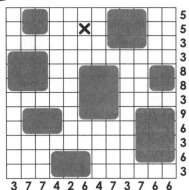

Column clues: 3 7 7 4 2 6 4 7 3 7 6 6

Row clues: 5 5 3 3 8 8 3 9 6 3 6 3

123 Loop
World-Class Puzzle #1
2010 Round 8

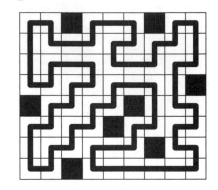

109 Japanese Sums
National Puzzle #2
2009 Round 12, Serkan Yürekli

(1~7)

| | | 1 | 14 | 6 | 12 | 8 | 12 | | 10 |
		27	8	1	2	4	5	28	3
7	15	1	4	2		5	3	7	
	28		7	3	4	2	1	6	5
10 7	9	7	3		6	1		5	4
2	8	2				4	3	1	
5	20	5		6	7	4	2	1	
3 5	8	3		5		6	2		
8	4	6	2				4		
13 5	3	4	6	1	2		5		3

Top clues: 5 10 4

114 Missing Skyscrapers
National Puzzle #1
2006 Round 6, Deyan Razsadov

(1~5)

Top clues: **2** **4** **4**

	5	4	3	2	•	1	**5**
2	•	1	5	3	4	2	
4	1	2	4	•	5	3	**2**
	4	5	2	1	3	•	
	3	•	1	4	2	5	**1**
3	2	3	•	5	1	4	

Bottom clues: **4** **4**

127 Domino Castle
World-Class Puzzle #1
2008 Round 2, A. Bogdanov

97 Boomerangs
National Puzzle
2008 Round 8, Vladimir Portugalov

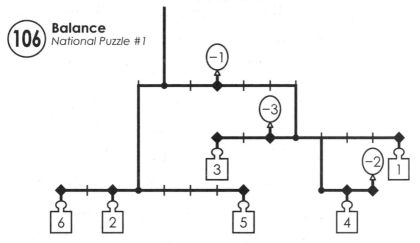

SOLUTIONS

106 Balance
National Puzzle #1

100 Minesweeper
National Puzzle #1
2004 Round 1

		2		●		0			
	●		●	2	2		2	2	
2				1		●		●	●
	●				2		2		2
		1		●			1		
			2		2	●			1
		●		0				2	●
	1							2	●
							2	●	2

144 Coins
World-Class Puzzle
2005 Round 5

(50¢)	(1¢)	(1¢)	(5¢)	(50¢)	$1.07
(5¢)	(50¢)	(25¢)	(25¢)	(50¢)	$1.55
($1)	(5¢)	(5¢)	(5¢)	(1¢)	$1.16
($1)	(5¢)	($1)	(10¢)	($1)	$3.15
(50¢)	(1¢)	($1)	(10¢)	(1¢)	$1.62
$3.05	62¢	$2.31	55¢	$2.02	

110 Easy as ABC
National Puzzle #1
2004 Round 1

```
    A B C C B B
  A · · · B · C
B · B · C A · · A
C · · C A · B · B
B · · B · C A · A
  B C A · · · · A
C C A · · · · B
B · · · B · C A
    C A A   C C
```

142 Tapa
World-Class Puzzle #1
2009 Round 10, Gülce Özkütük

183

(154) Missing Skyscrapers
World-Class Puzzle #1
2006 Round 6, Deyan Razsadov

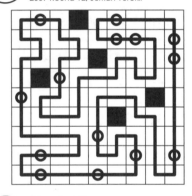

(105) Zero Kakuro
National Puzzle
2003 Finals

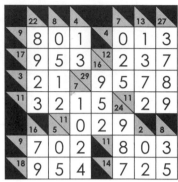

(124) Loop
World-Class Puzzle #2
2009 Round 12, Serkan Yürekli

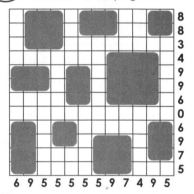

(132) Clouds
World-Class Puzzle #1
2008 Round 11, Andrey Bogdanov

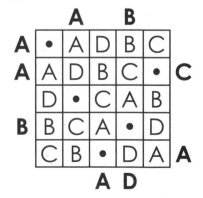

(156) Star Battle
World-Class Puzzle #1
2003 Round 15

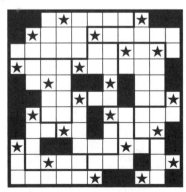

(111) Easy as ABC
National Puzzle #2
2007 Round 4, Ricardo Daniel Kossatz

147 Balance
World-Class Puzzle #2
2004 Round 9

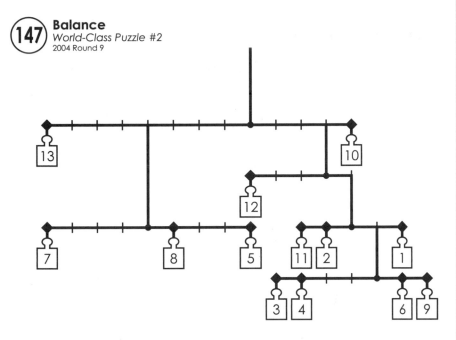

128 Domino Castle
World-Class Puzzle #2
2005 Round 1

185

(133) Clouds
World-Class Puzzle #2
2004 Round 1

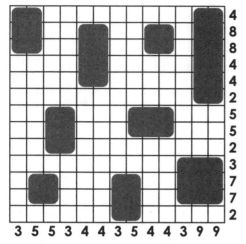

4 8 8 4 4 2 5 5 2 3 7 7 2

3 5 5 3 4 4 3 5 4 4 3 9 9

(117) Star Battle
National Puzzle #2
2004 Finals

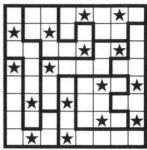

(125) Loop
World-Class Puzzle #3
2007 Finals, Daniel Martin

136 Ones and Fives
World-Class Puzzle
2006 Round 1, Deyan Razsadov

103 Tapa
National Puzzle #2
2010 Round 8

153 Ikebana
World-Class Puzzle
2009 Team Finals, Serkan Yürekli

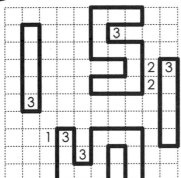

112 Easy as ABC
National Puzzle #3
2007 Round 14, Daniel Martin

140 Minesweeper
World-Class Puzzle
2006 Round 9, Deyan Razsadov

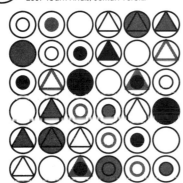

107 Balance
National Puzzle #2
2006 Round 11, Deyan Razsadov

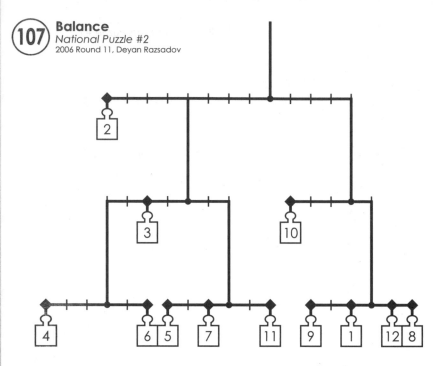

145 Zero Kakuro
World-Class Puzzle
2004 Finals

138 Nurikabe
World-Class Puzzle #1
2008 Round 7, Olga Leontieva

148 Japanese Sums
World-Class Puzzle #1
2005 Round 11

(1~7)			4					6	17
	9	12	11	16	12	4	14	2	
	10	11	8	12	8	13	5	4	
4 3 13	4		1	2				6	7
25 1	5	6	3	4	7				1
2 22		2		6	5	1	7	3	
14 14	2	4	7	1		3	5	6	
7 8 2	7		4	3	1		2		
8 9 2	1	7			4	5		2	
23		1	2	7	3	6	4		
14 7		3	6	5		2	1	4	

104 Coins
National Puzzle
2005 Round 5

25¢	1¢	$1	25¢	1¢	$1.52
5¢	1¢	$1	$1	1¢	$2.07
5¢	10¢	$1	10¢	5¢	$1.30
$1	1¢	50¢	50¢	1¢	$2.02
25¢	1¢	25¢	10¢	5¢	66¢
$1.60	14¢	$3.75	$1.95	13¢	

155 Missing Skyscrapers
World-Class Puzzle #2
2006 Round 6, Deyan Razsadov

(1~5)	3		3		3		
	1	5	2	4	3	•	3
3	3	4	•	5	1	2	
	5	3	4	•	2	1	4
4	•	1	3	2	4	5	1
	4	2	5	1	•	3	2
3	2	•	1	3	5	4	
	3	4	2	2			

150 Easy as ABC
World-Class Puzzle #1
2008 Round 2, A. Fabris, A. Bogdanov

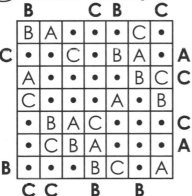

118 Star Battle
National Puzzle #3
2006 Semi-finals 1, Deyan Razsadov

189

101 Minesweeper
National Puzzle #2
2007 Round 8
Guilherme M. dos Santos Silva

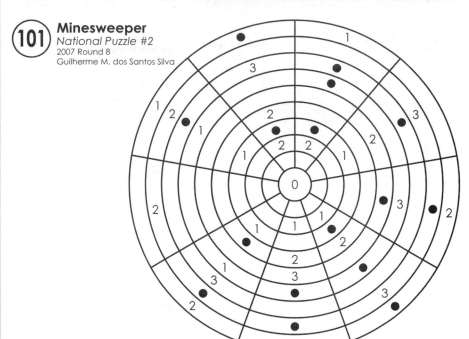

146 Balance
World-Class Puzzle #1
2007 Round 13, Ricardo Daniel Kossatz

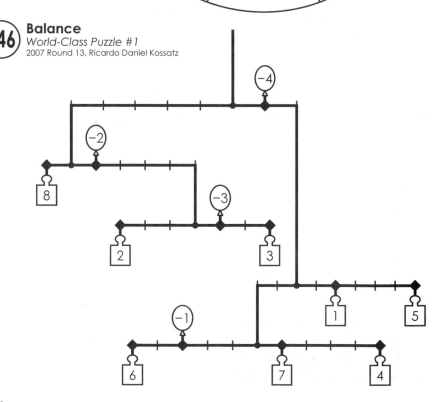

(115) Missing Skyscrapers
National Puzzle #2
2006 Round 6, Deyan Razsadov

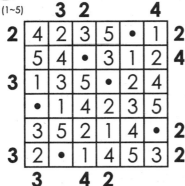

(1~5)

	3	2			4		
2	4	2	3	5	•	1	2
	5	4	•	3	1	2	4
3	1	3	5	•	2	4	
	•	1	4	2	3	5	
	3	5	2	1	4	•	2
3	2	•	1	4	5	3	2
	3		4	2			

(139) Nurikabe
World-Class Puzzle #2
2000 Round 8, vDave Tuller

(149) Japanese Sums
World-Class Puzzle #2
2003 Round 5

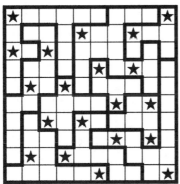

(143) Tapa
World-Class Puzzle #2
2009 Round 10, Gülce Özkütük

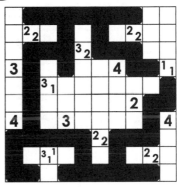

(158) Star Battle
World-Class Puzzle #3
2006 Semi-finals 2, Vladimir Portugalov

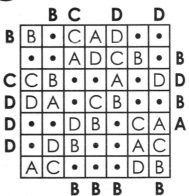

(151) Easy as ABC
World-Class Puzzle #2
2007 Round 4, Ricardo Daniel Kossatz

	B	C		D		D		
B	B	•	C	A	D	•	•	
	•	•	A	D	C	B	•	B
C	C	B	•	•	A	•	D	D
D	D	A	•	C	B	•	•	B
D	•	•	D	B	•	C	A	A
D	•	D	B	•	•	A	C	
	A	C	•	•	•	D	B	
	B	B	B		B			

(113) Ikebana
National Puzzle

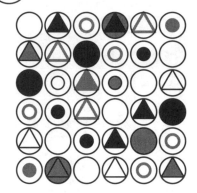

(152) Easy as ABC
World-Class Puzzle #3
2009 Round 3, Deren Çaᐧlayan

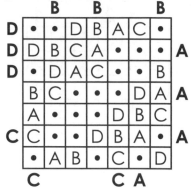

(157) Star Battle
World-Class Puzzle #2
2008 Round 6, Vladimir Portugalov

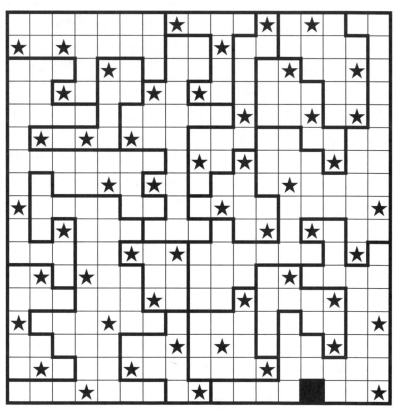

Tutorials
& Hints

Loop, Training Puzzle #2 (page 8):

To get started on Loop puzzles, it helps to realize that every white cell has four borders, and exactly two will be used by the loop and two will not. So, you can draw segments of the loop at the "corners" and "tunnels," where the cells already have two edges that can't be used by the loop.

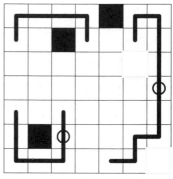

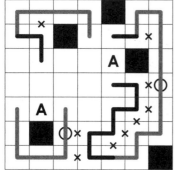

Once you've determined some edges, it can be helpful to mark the edges of the cells that are *not* part of the loop. This can help you find more "corners" and "tunnels."

Spots adjacents to two ends of the same loop segment, like the cells marked "A" above, can be useful. There are only three ways to have the loop go through the cell, but since you can't close the loop early, one of those ways doesn't work. This forces one of the edges to be used.

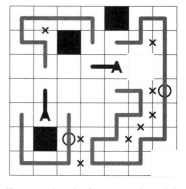

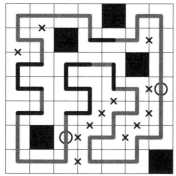

Repeating these techniques should allow you to make substantial progress, if not completely solve, all the Loop puzzles in this book.

Domino Castle, Training Puzzle #1 (page 15):

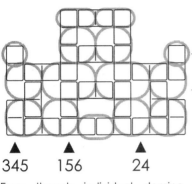

◀246

◀1235

One of the first things to do is to find and mark "clusters" of domino halves that all have to be the same digit. You can find these by seeing where dominoes touch each other.

▲ 345   ▲ 156   ▲ 24

Even though individual domino halves may not be pointed at by arrows in both directions, the same cluster may be pointed at and can help you put some digits in. Also, a row, like the 1235 row here, has only four clusters, which means that each cluster has a different number.

A = 3 or 5
B = 1 or 5
C = 3 or 5

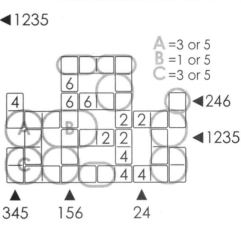

◀246

◀1235

▲ 345   ▲ 156   ▲ 24

Another useful rule is that "two clusters touching the same cluster cannot have the same digit." In the diagram above, B and C both touch A, so they can't have the same number; otherwise AB and AC would reuse the same domino. Using that information, we can deduce that B is not 5.

A = 3 or 5
C = 5 or 3
D = 3 or 5

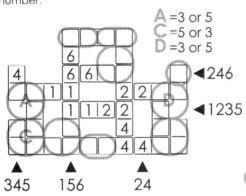

◀246

◀1235

▲ 345   ▲ 156   ▲ 24

It's also good to count the total number of domino halves with the same digit. In this puzzle, each digit is used exactly seven times. This means that 5 can't be in D, since it would have to be used in C as well as the 156 column, which is too many times.

Repeating these rules and keeping good track of which dominoes are used should help you finish off this puzzle.

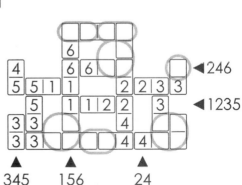

◀246

◀1235

▲ 345   ▲ 156   ▲ 24

195

Clouds, Training Puzzle #2 (page 26):

Since every cloud is at least two long in both directions, it means that "2" and "3" clues are always just one single cloud, and that if they are next to each other, they are separate. This allows you to draw a "barrier" where you know no cloud can cross.

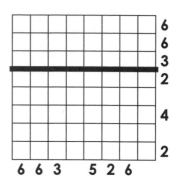

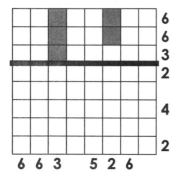

The "3" in the third row must be one cloud, and that cloud must therefore use up 3 of the "6" in the second row. This in turns means that the top two rows must have the "6"s split into two 3s (so the top three rows have a 3×3 and a 3×2).

The "3" and the "2" column then force some knowledge of the cells, and then diagonal and count constraints give even more information. It can also help to try to write "sum breakdown" possibilities for the larger numbers.

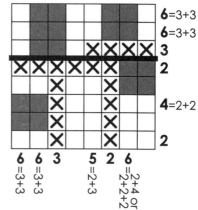

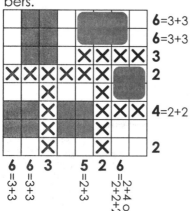

In this case, the "5" column being a 2+3 forces the 4 row pretty quickly, getting you very close to the end of the puzzle.

Tapa, Training Puzzle #1 (page 45):

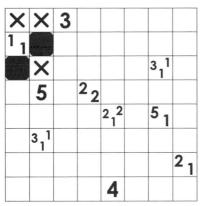

Knowing that the wall is completely contiguous allows you to start at the upper-left. You can deduce that neither of the first two cells in the first row can be wall parts, since for them to get out and connect with the rest of the land you would need to violate the "1,1" cell rule. This allows you to determine the surrounding bits of the "1,1" cell immediately.

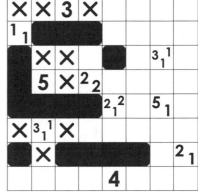

Now more information comes from the "3" and the "5" constraints, and you can also in turn deduce the "3,1,1" group in the lower-left, as well as get partial information on the "2,2" and the "4."

The lower-left wall segments needs to connect, and that with the 2-by-2 constraint forces out the "4." More importantly, the "5" wall segment coming out determines one of the 2s in the "2,2,1" group. If you run through the possible ways to do the "2,2,1" now, you'll realize that two wall segments are determined, while exactly one of the two cells labeled "A" is a wall.

This means that the "north" wall and the "south" wall can't connect through the "A" passage, which means that they have to connect through the "B" passage, and so all the "B" cells are walls. This in turn forces the "5,1" group, and that means that the "C" cells are also walls, which will force the "3,1,1" group. You should be able to handle the rest of the puzzle by yourself from here.

Hints

Loop, Training Puzzle #6 (page 12): If the lower-right of your puzzle looks like the diagram at right, it's worth noting that if the circle has a vertical path going through it, then the loop will prematurely close up.

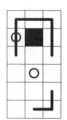

Domino Castle, Training Puzzle #4 (page 18): Each number can only appear in an even number of odd-sized clusters.

Nurikabe, Training Puzzle #2 (page 38): There are not many places where the "5" island can go.

Minesweeper, Training Puzzle #2 (page 42): Look at the 3 and 1 next to each other in the third row from the top. There must be at least two mines that are next to the 3 that aren't next to the 1. Where must they be? (Finding similar pairs is the key to solving Minesweeper puzzles.)

Zero Kakuro, Training Puzzle #1 (page 51): The nine cells in the lower-left have a total sum of 6+17+9. Subtract the seven cells in the lower-left, which have a total sum of 4+22+4, and you'll be left with the sum of the other two cells.

Star Battle, Training Puzzle #3 (page 75): The bottom two rows are completely within two regions. That means that the stars in those rows account for all the stars in those regions, hence anything in those regions that aren't in those rows can't have stars. (This rule is useful for more than just this Star Battle, by the way.)

Star Battle, Training Puzzle #6 (page 78): Here's an advanced technique. In the diagram to the right, suppose you know that there is a star in one of the cells marked A and there is a star in one of the cells marked B. Then there can't be any star in the cell marked X. Do you see why?

Domino Castle, National Puzzle #1 (page 87): There are only two clusters that are "odd" (that is, have an odd number of half-dominoes in them). Anything you can deduce from that?

Hints

Domino Castle, National Puzzle #2 (page 88): Each digit appears seven times, which means each digit appears in exactly 1 or 3 odd-sized clusters. But there are only eight odd-sized clusters...

Minesweeper, National Puzzle #1 (page 100): In the diagram on the right, the given numbers add up to exactly 13. Hmm....

Star Battle, National Puzzle #2 (page 117): This puzzle is a bit of a "trick puzzle." It turns out that on an 8×8 grid there are only two possible Star Battle solutions, no matter how you draw the regions.

	2						
			2		2		
		1					
			2			1	
1							
							2

Domino Castle, World-Class Puzzle #1 (page 127): There are only two places the double-zero domino can go, and if you look hard enough, one of them won't work.

Coins, World-Class Puzzle (page 144): For each row, ask yourself the question: "How many quarters can be in this row?"

Zero Kakuro, World-Class Puzzle (page 145): After solving the lower-right, stretching left and up, and putting in three numbers in the upper-left, you might find yourself unable to see what to do next. It turns out that the "5" in the upper-right is more restricted than it might seem.

Star Battle, World-Class Puzzle #3 (page 158): Sorry, this last puzzle is just insanely hard to do without trial-and-error. We know of only one person who has maanged to do it, and that after a few hours!

Puzzle Index

A Note About the Type

This book is wholly set in Century Gothic, a geometric sans-serif typeface designed for Monotype Imaging in 1991. Its crisp geometric curves allow it to be perfectly suited for logic puzzles while still maintaining a distinctive look. It was the official typeface used for the 4th World Sudoku Championship in 2010.